ANNE SCOTT PLUMMER

INTERVIEW BY **Viola Frey**

ESSAY BY **Martha Drexler Lynn**

EDITED BY **William Bartman**

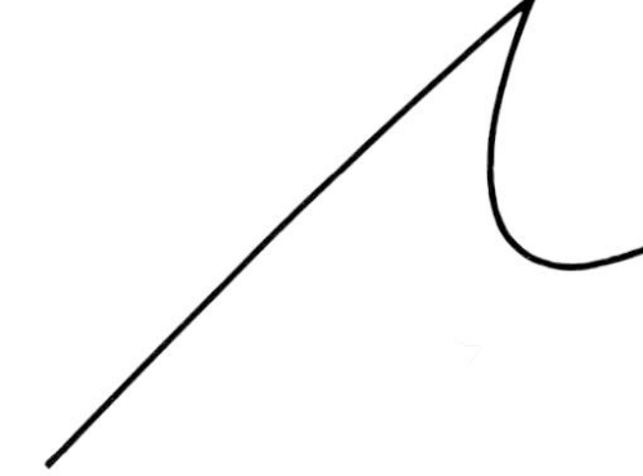

© 1989 W.S.B. Foundation
Design:
Lausten/Cossutta Design
Copy Editing:
Joseph N. Newland
Photography:
Charles Allen
Rob Corning
Janice Felgar
Anne Scott Plummer
Kohler Company
John Michael Kohler Arts Center
Ron Faranovich
Gary Colby
Chris Felver
Grey Crawford
Typesetting:
Continental Typographics
Printing:
Gardner Lithograph

For information regarding
A.R.T. Press, contact:
W.S.B. Foundation
8501 Wilshire Boulevard
Suite 250
Beverly Hills, California 90211

ISBN 0-923183-02-7

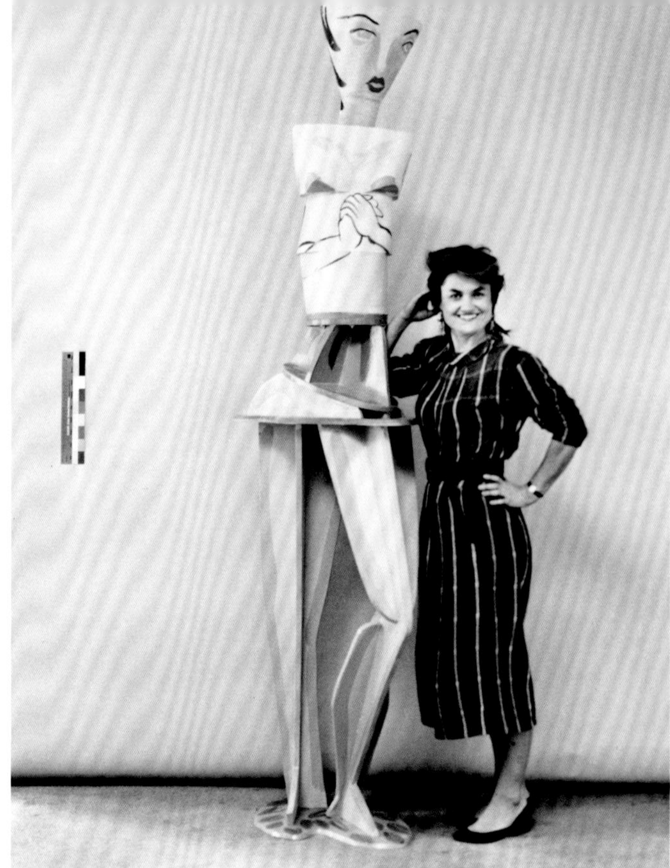

Anne Scott Plummer with Inès, 1988
Ceramic and wood with acrylic
Height, 92 in.

ANNE SCOTT PLUMMER

Interviewed by Viola Frey

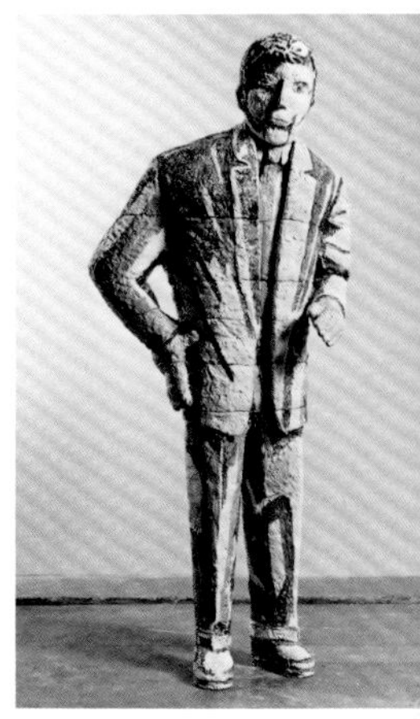

Viola Frey
Hand-out Man, 1985
Ceramic with glazes
110 x 56 x 36 in.
Courtesy of the artist and Asher/
Faure, Los Angeles

Viola Frey teaches at the California College of Arts and Crafts. "My work is large-scale urban figures, clothed and naked, that neither condemns nor approves what is going on in this world."

Viola Frey Have you always worked in clay?

ANNE SCOTT PLUMMER From the time I was a little kid I was always interested in painting. Both my parents went to the Rhode Island School of Design — my mother was working on an art education degree and my father was studying textiles there. That was when Rhode Island was a big textile manufacturing state. The story my parents tell of how they met is that my mother hung up some of her watercolors and they dripped on my father's dyed yarns....So when I was a kid, my mother, who never completed her degree, always encouraged me to do art projects. She remained a Sunday painter. I would paint using the leftovers on her palette. I was also fascinated by the figure drawings which she had done when she was in school.

I won first prize in a local art show when I was twelve or thirteen, and my mother won second prize for her painting. When they told me I had won first prize, I assumed it was in the youth category, but I was astounded, then gratified, to find out that I was considered an adult. Since then I've considered myself an artist.

Frey How did you get started working with clay?

PLUMMER In high school I made my first painted sculpture. It was a formed canvas, three-dimensional. There was something about that which really struck me: this painted sculpture. I think that I had never really thought of it before, having something three-dimensional, sculptural, and being able to paint it as well. That's one of the things still fascinating to me about ceramics. That combination of painting and sculpture is so natural, so integrated. Clay looks right when it is glazed. It doesn't look as if you've applied paint on something three-dimensional, it looks as if it's all one material.

Nevertheless, my father didn't think it was such a good idea to go to art school. It was in the late sixties and the people at Rhode Island School of Design were walking around barefoot with torn jeans and all, and that didn't make a big impression on him. So I just chucked the whole thing. I'd go to art school later.

Frey What did you do then?

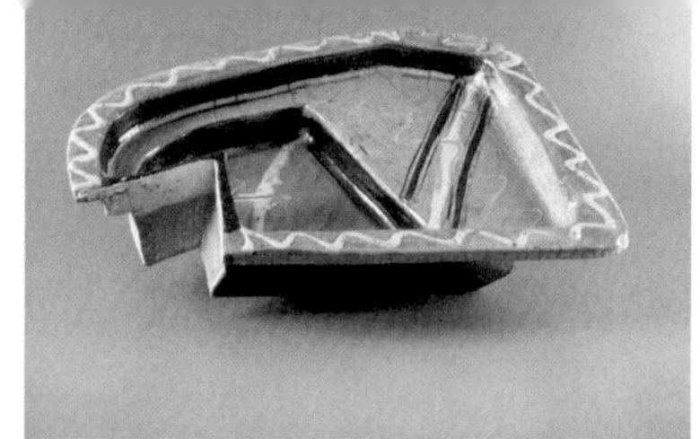
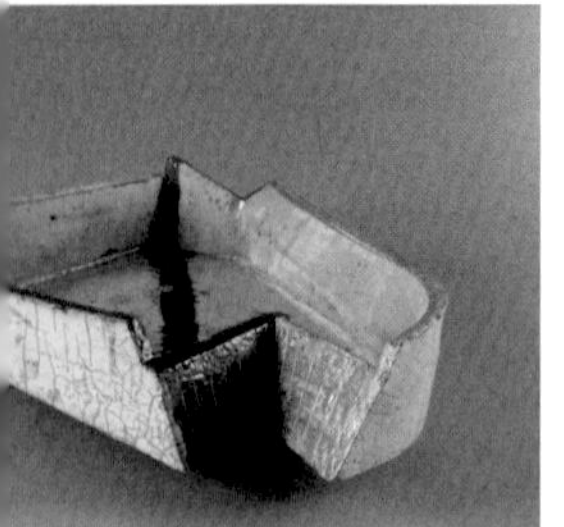
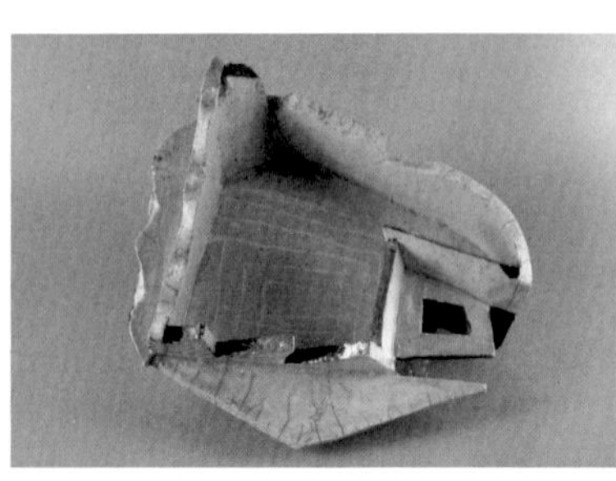
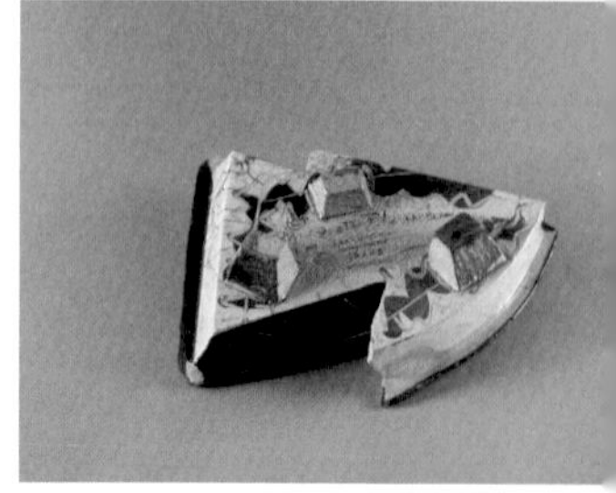
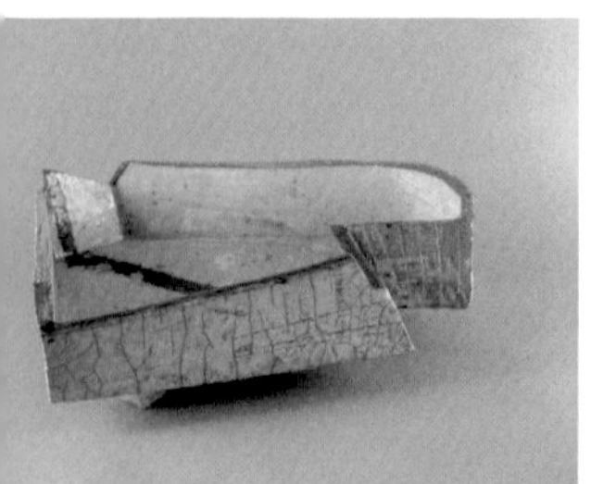
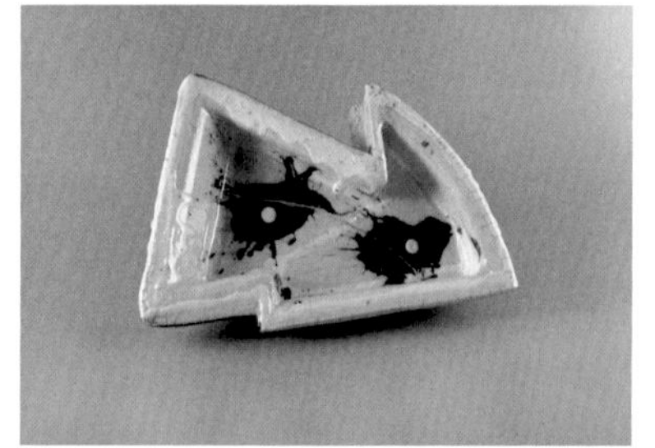
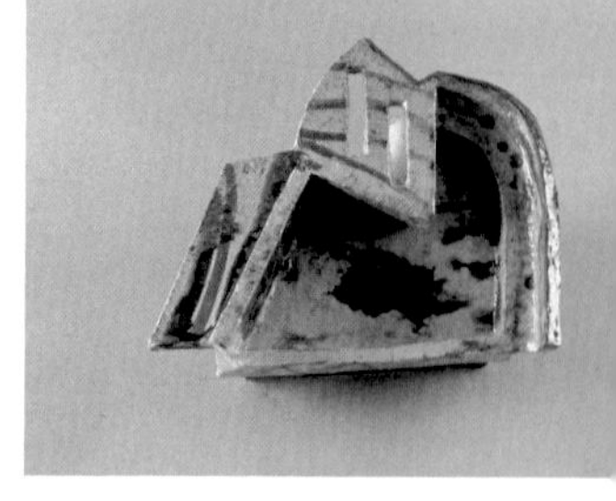
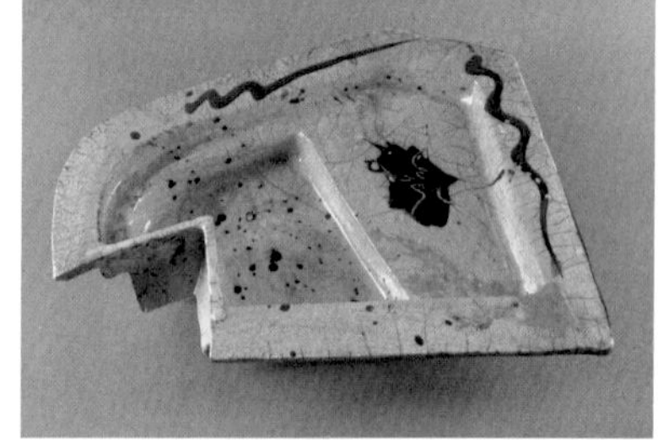
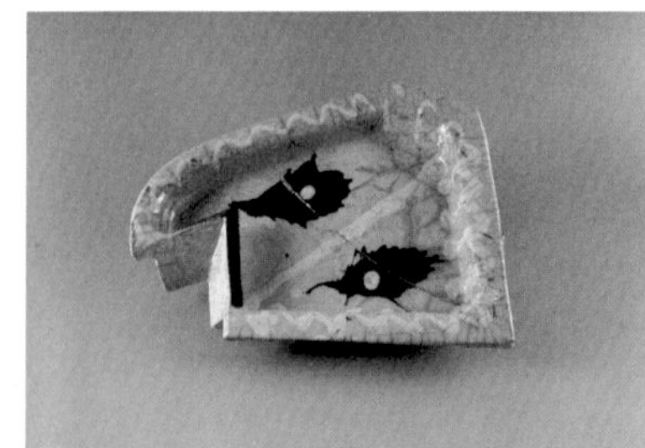
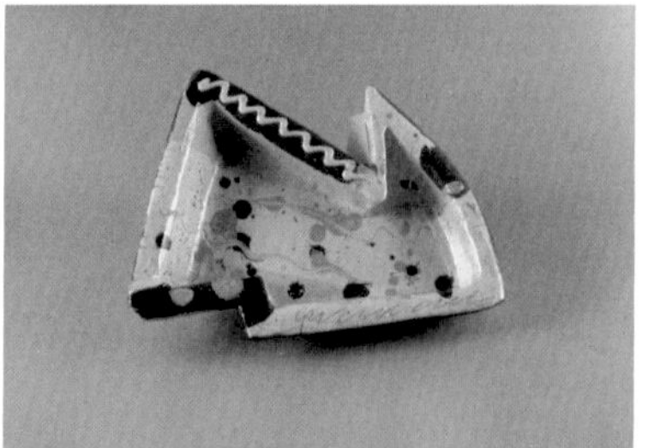
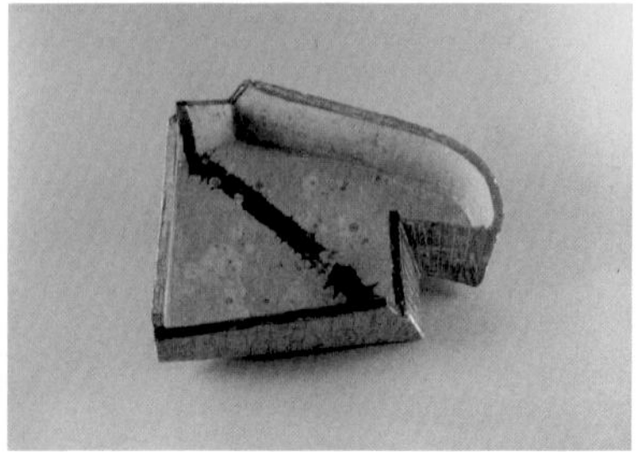
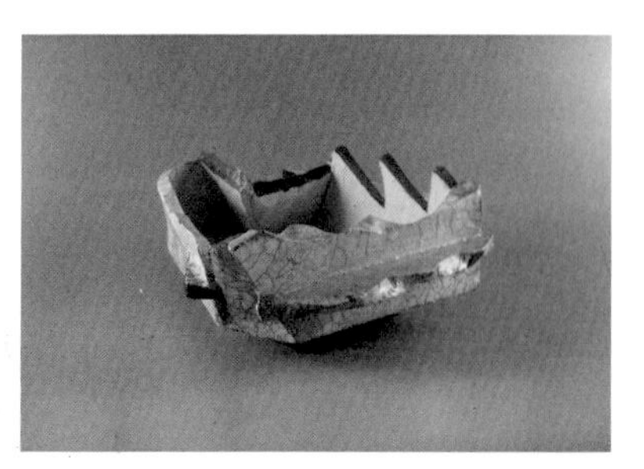

PLUMMER I took a brief side trip as an air traffic controller in the Air Force. I was rebelling. It was a way to be independent from my family, to get away from their control.

Frey Being an artist wasn't enough of a rebellion?

PLUMMER I guess not. After the service and before I went to Rhode Island School of Design I lived in Provincetown on Cape Cod for four years. I had a painting studio there and started to make pots to earn my living. I worked as a carpenter in the wintertime. In the summer I got together with a potter and learned how to make pots. I thought it was a great way to earn a living, and that was really my first introduction to ceramics. I didn't think of it as fine art. I sort of painted on the surface of these pots.

I also socialized with artists and I modeled for artists, so I saw people working. These were artists who worked at the Provincetown workshop. It gave me an opportunity to watch serious, young artists working: painting, sketching and hanging their exhibitions. I had always thought I was a natural-born artist and didn't need to go to school. But after awhile I realized that there were things I could learn in school.

My first year at Rhode Island School of Design was a real breakthrough for me. In that first year, the freshman foundation year, we explored a lot of different materials, and the whole idea of combining materials seemed natural after these experiences. I loved it and I stayed up all night doing lots of projects because it was such a welcome challenge.

John Gill was one of the people who worked with clay in a real sensitive way that had an effect on me. Up until then I had been working with people who had this aggressive, the bigger-the-better attitude toward working with clay. John Gill was a big man but he had a very subtle, sensitive approach to the material. Jackie Rice was the head of the department the last two years I was there. She was very inspiring to me because she exposed me to the work of many contemporary ceramic artists and to their ideas. She really elevated my perception of working with clay as a fine art material.

Frey Now you're a California artist — how did you make the transition from there to here?

PLUMMER Well, I came here to go to graduate school. I came out to Claremont without having been to Southern California. I packed up all my things into a drive-away car and took off across the country. Just that experience alone was great. I love to travel, and there is something wonderful about driving cross-country. You really know what ground you've covered.

I worked with Paul Soldner at Claremont. That was who I came out to study with. I had read an article about him in *Ceramics Monthly* that made me realize he was an important artist and someone that I wanted to be involved with. Soldner really teaches by example; he emphasizes an intuitive approach; he does things because they feel right. Roland Reiss is another artist I worked with in Claremont. He is intellectual and conceptual in his approach to art, and this balanced with Soldner's more personal, value-oriented approach. The

Opposite
ORIBE COWGIRL SERIES, 1980
Raku-fired ceramic with glazes
Length or diameter, 12 in.
Made at Sun Valley Center of Arts and Humanities
Below
From a sketchbook, 1980

other great thing about Claremont is that there are fifty grad students, so there are lots of people to talk to. My work really started to develop in graduate school.

Frey Other than these professors, what else has inspired you in your work?

PLUMMER The other thing that inspired me was my uncle, Galway Kinnell, who is a well-known poet. When I was a child there was a certain disapproval expressed by the family because he wasn't well known when I was young. He was struggling. He was very involved in the civil rights movement and his poetry reflected that. He sort of just got by financially. The little information I got about the things he thought about made a big impression on me. He gave us things like a book of the stars, the constellations, and he talked about the stories behind them, the myths that they illustrate. He brought me a penknife that he said was the kind of knife that art students in Paris used to sharpen their drawing pencils, and that was one of my prized possessions for a long time. Of course my mother didn't think I was old enough to have a knife. I was a little kid then. I thought his lifestyle was fascinating and exotic. He traveled a lot and thought about different things than I was exposed to. He was involved with the world at large, not just the small community that I called home.

Frey I see... You did a series of pieces about Sun Valley. What was that all about?

PLUMMER I first went to Sun Valley in the summer of 1980 as a graduate student. One of the other students was associated with Sun Valley Center of Arts and Humanities. It sounded great to me so I went there. It's a ski resort in the winter and it's really beautiful in the summer. It's up in the mountains, there's still snow on the peaks, and it's cool and green.

I went up there as a student that one summer, and I went back two other times as an artist-in-residence. The first time I went back, in 1983, I did the kiln pieces. They had recently built a big wood-fired kiln and were doing a few firings in it. It's a big communal project firing a wood kiln up. All the wood has to be chopped into small pieces and the whole thing gets loaded with the work of maybe fifteen people. Then there's the firing, which involves constant stoking and monitoring of the smoke coming out, constant adjustments, and the continuous chopping of wood. This is an all-day/all-night project. I got involved in it and I fired a few pieces in that kiln. It got me thinking about how closely ceramic artists are associated with the technology of kilns — what a symbiotic relationship there is between the ceramic artist and this kind of magical process of firing, so I did five or six pieces that explored the relationship between the artist and the technology of firing. The largest one was *Spirit of the Wood Kiln* (page 12). It was an image of that big kiln with bright red, drippy, fiery glaze. On the outside I drew images of the whole work process, all the manual labor involved in loading up and firing the kiln. It had a head coming out of the top that represented the spirit of the kiln because kilns seem to have their own

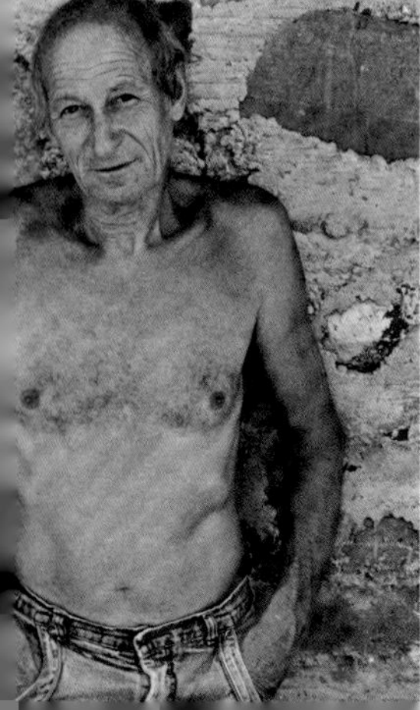

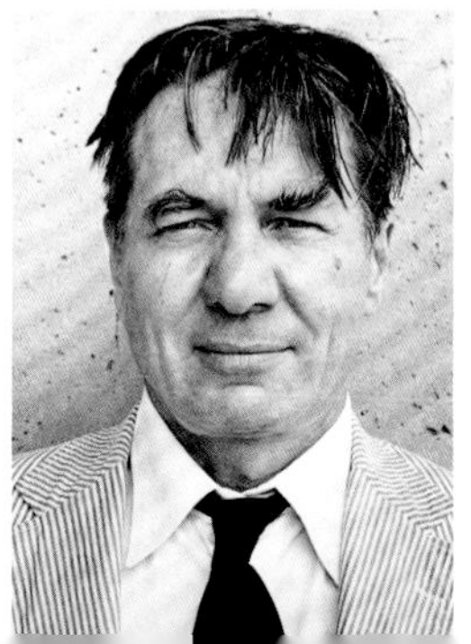

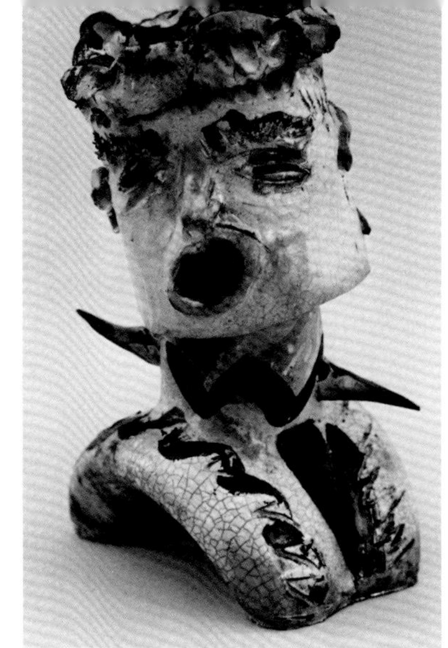

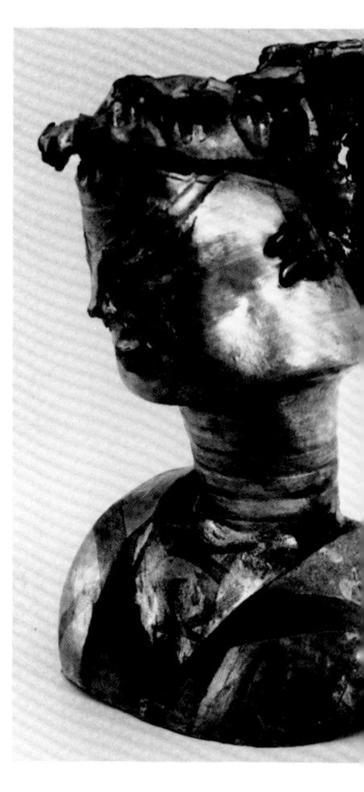

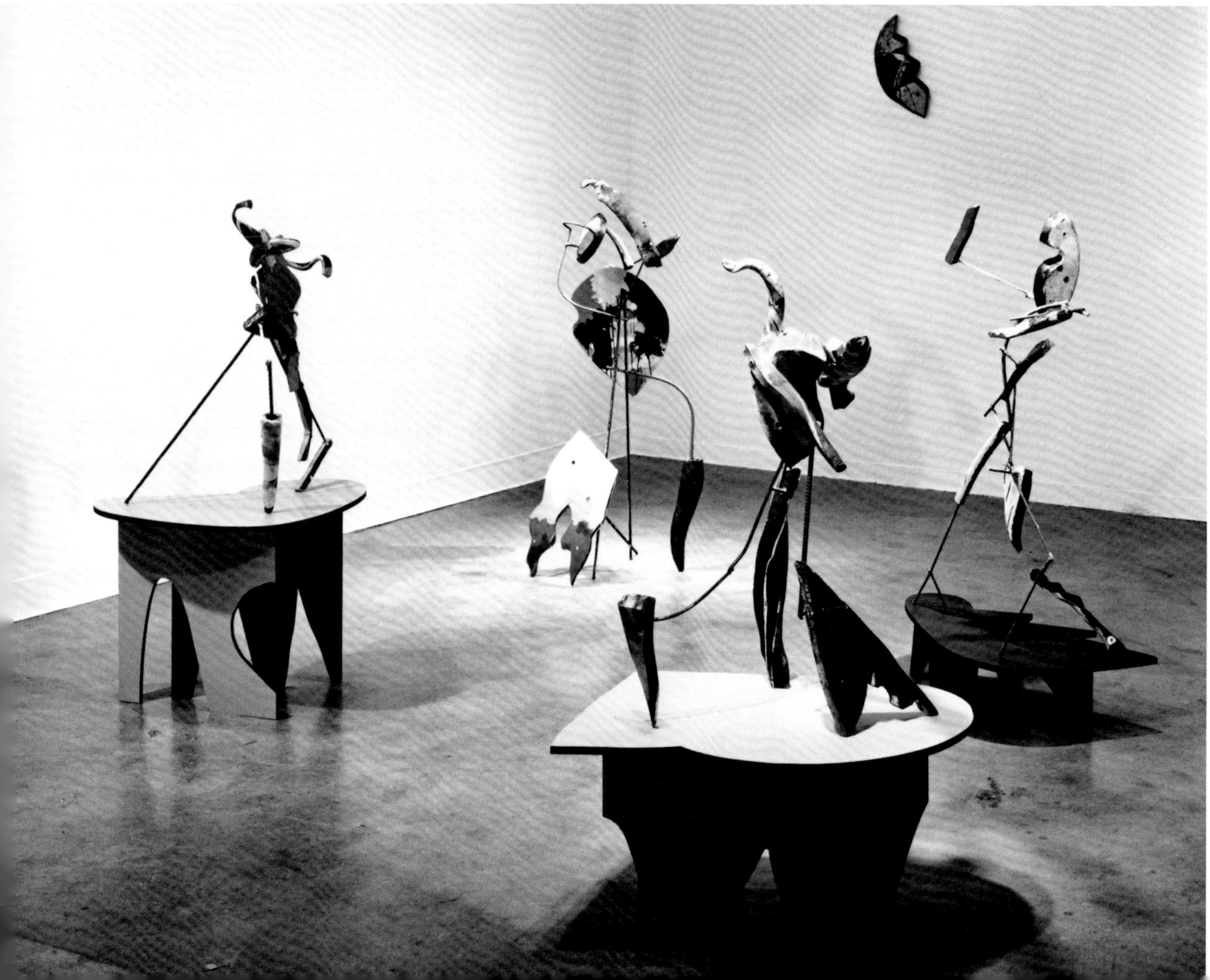

I had ten boxes and you're only allowed three, including luggage, I put everything on the train very early before any conductors were around. I was advised, "Get it on the train before they know you have too much." I had to take two trips in a taxi to get it to the station, and when I arrived there were no porters around, but I still got all the boxes on. As the train started off, one of the first things that they said was that the train would be separating. The front half of the train was going to Frankfurt and the other half was going somewhere else. I enlisted the help of a couple of young women who spoke a little bit of English. I asked them if they would claim the pieces as their own when we went across the border because I had too much. They said sure, they'd do that. Then I asked them if they would mind helping me carry the boxes up to the front half of the train. So, one at a time, we carried these big boxes through the narrow little aisles. Between each car there were about four doors — vacuum shut doors. It was a big deal to open them, squeeze through the door and get on to the next, and then, of course, we bumped into every single person along the aisle to the right part of the train. Then we had to find places to store all these boxes, and of course everyone had put their luggage up on the luggage racks. Well, we had about two and a half hours. When we got to the biggest box, it wouldn't go through the doors. There was a stop just before the train was to separate. It was a sixty-second stop. I said, "Look, we're gonna have to run outside the train with this box. We've got sixty seconds to run the length of the train, and then we'll jump back on the other end." The conductors were warning us to remain seated unless it was our destination. In spite of the warning we jumped off the train with the box, two of us because it was oversized and heavy, and ran down to the other end and jumped back up on just before the train started up again — with us kind of hanging off. Then the train split up.

The next ordeal was the German customs officials: "What's all this? What are you going to do with it?" I don't speak any German and they didn't speak any English. Fortunately, one of the girls who had helped me spoke German and interpreted.

"What's the work?"

"It's art."

"How valuable is it?"

"Oh, not valuable at all."

"Then why are you bringing here?"

"Well, I'm just bringing it to my cousin."

"What are you going to do with it? Are you going to sell it?"

" Oh, no. I wouldn't think of selling it. In fact it's not even finished yet. Look, look at it."

And it's true — it wasn't finished. It wasn't even glazed. They didn't have glazes at the Ecole des Beaux-Arts. Jeanclous didn't use glazes so he figured that nobody else needed to either. Anyway, with the help of this girl I didn't have to pay any customs duties, but they had to rip open all the boxes to look at the contents and see that they were actually worthless pieces of art.

Matador Beach, California, 1985
Promotional photo session for use
during work at the Ecole des
Beaux-Arts, Paris, France

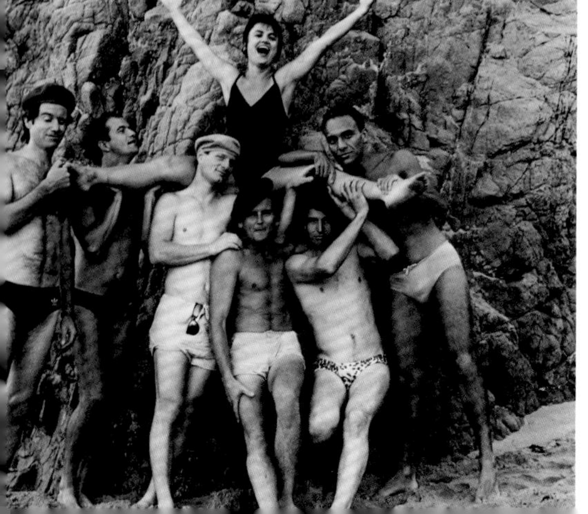

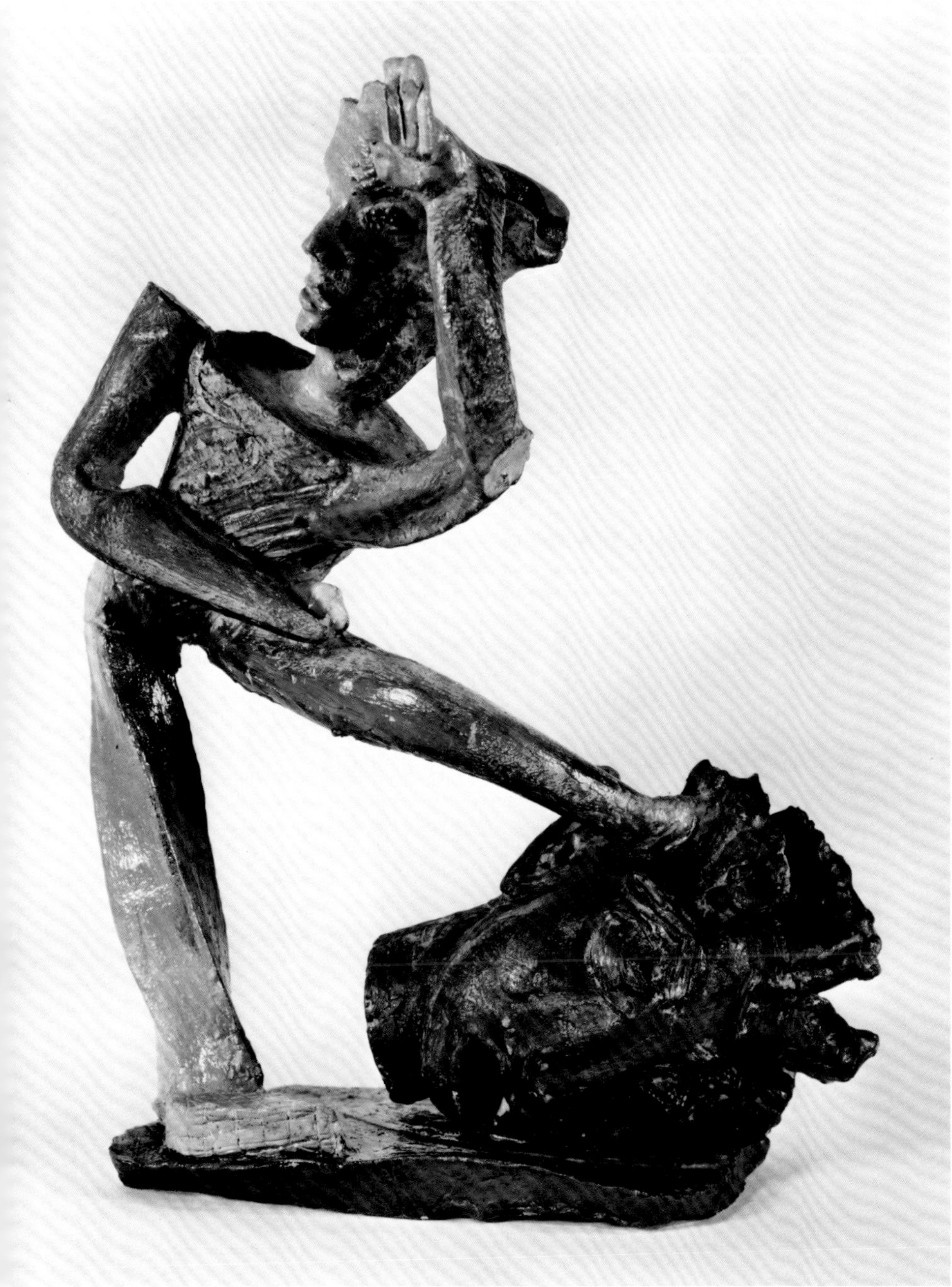

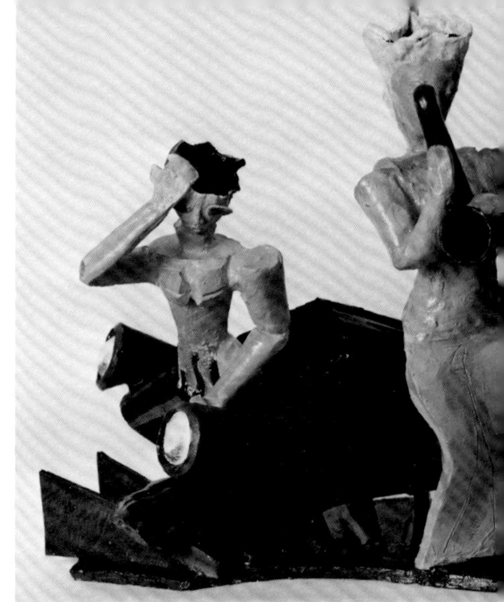

Above
Saxophone Muse, 1985
Low-fire ceramic with
acrylic
18 x 17 x 14 in.
Made at the Ecole des
Beaux-Arts, Paris, France
Left
David and Goliath, 1985
Low-fire ceramic with
acrylic
19 x 15 x 9 in.
Made at the Ecole des
Beaux-Arts

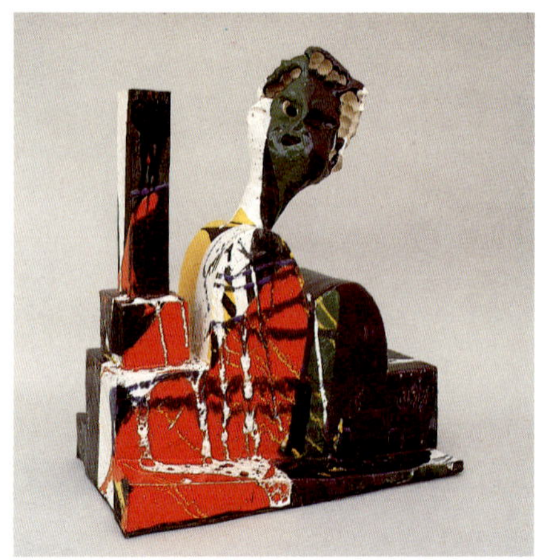 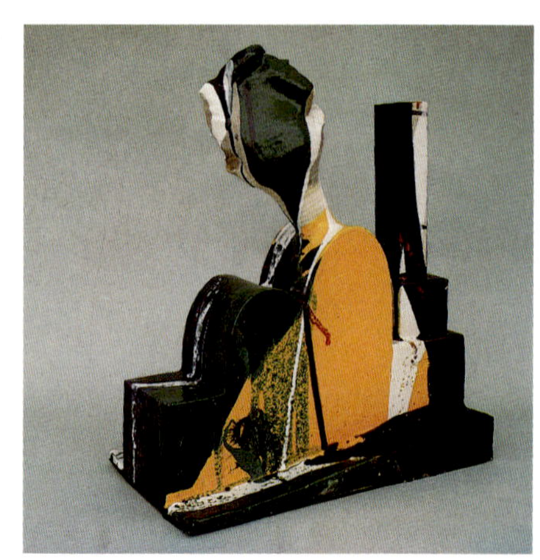

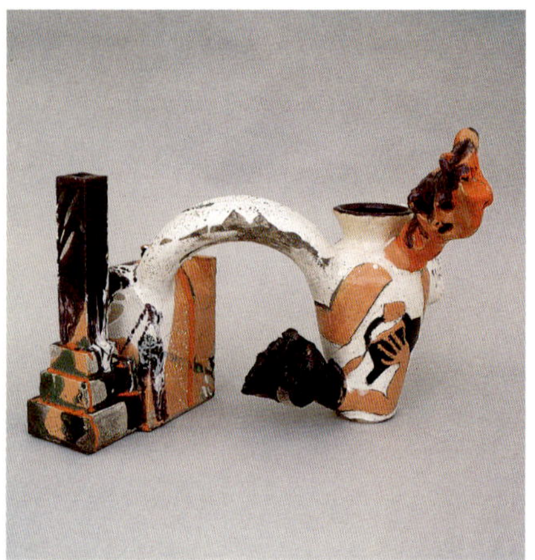 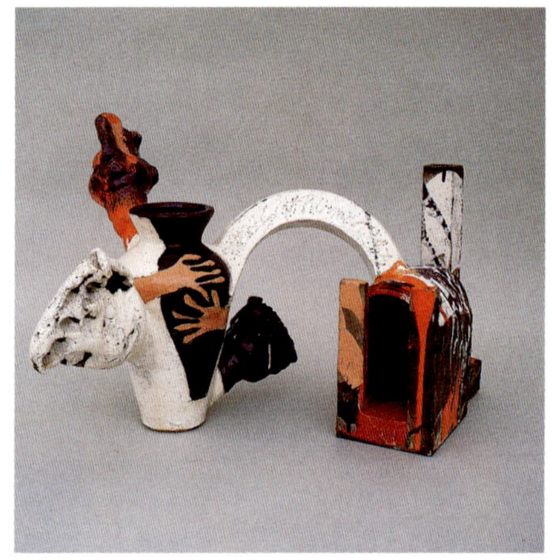

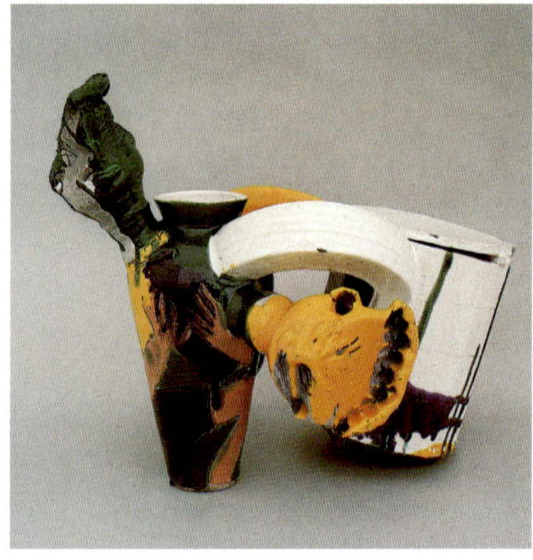 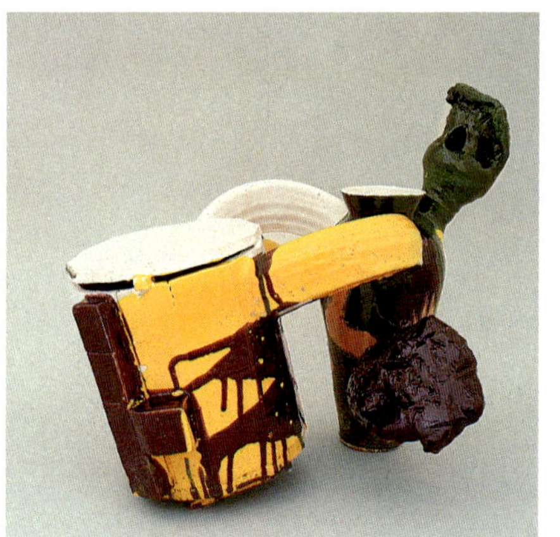

Top
SPIRIT OF THE WOOD KILN,
1983
Low-fire ceramic with
glazes
22 x 19 x 11 in.
Made at the Sun Valley
Center for Arts and
Humanities, Sun Valley,
Idaho
Middle
SUN VALLEY SALTY DOG, 1983
Low-fire ceramic with
glazes
15 x 24 x 15 in.
Made at the Sun Valley
Center for Arts and
Humanities
Right
SUN VALLEY MOUNTAIN MOMMA,
1983
Low-fire ceramic with
glazes
20 x 14 x 12 in.
Made at the Sun Valley
Center for Arts and
Humanities

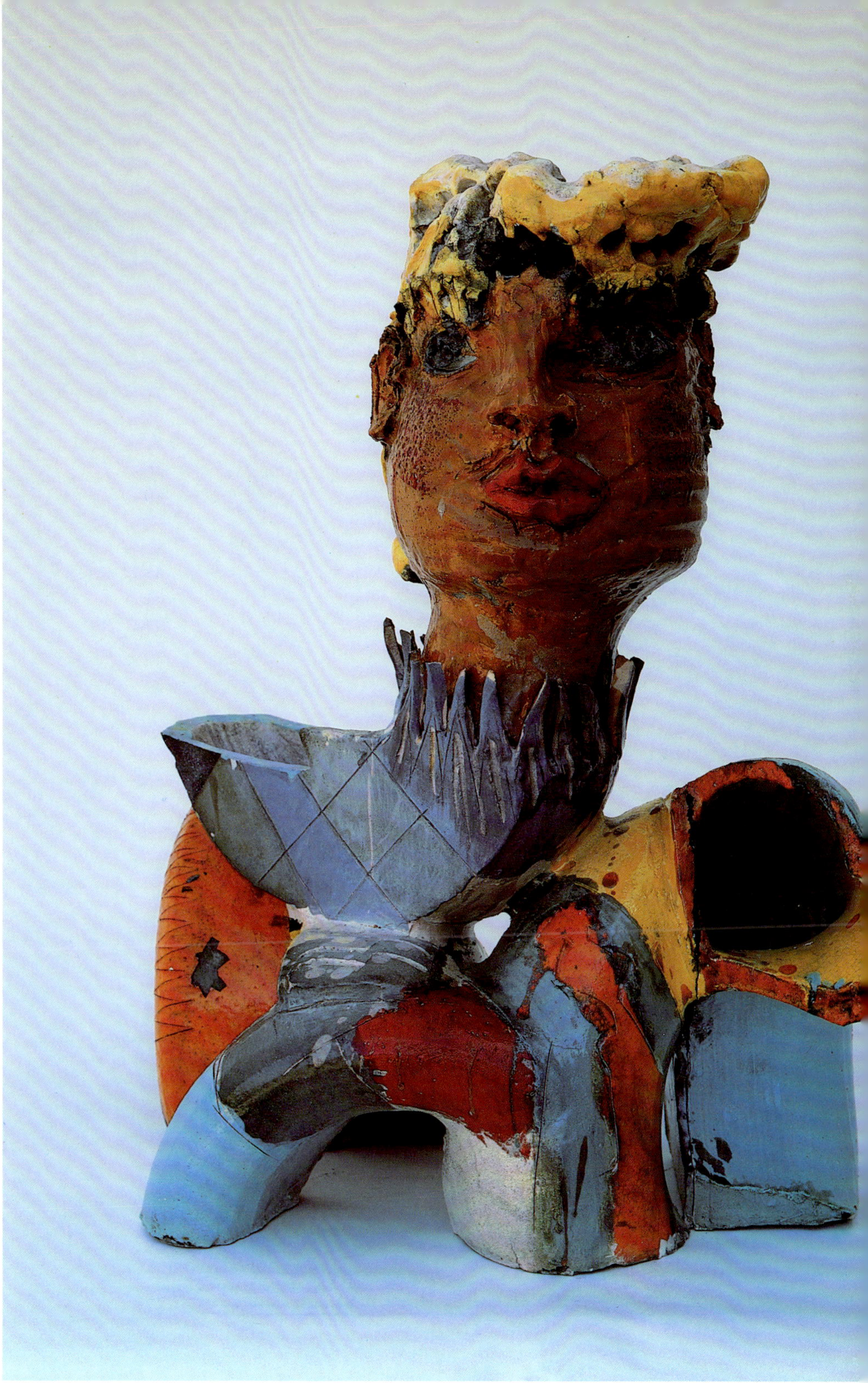

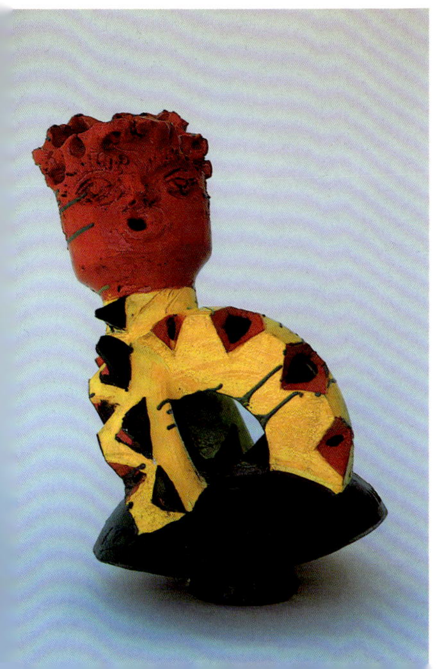

Above
ZIM BEET, 1982
Low-fire ceramic with
glazes
31 x 28 x 17 in.
Left
CHINESE SONG, 1984
Low-fire ceramic with
glazes
22 x 14 x 12 in.

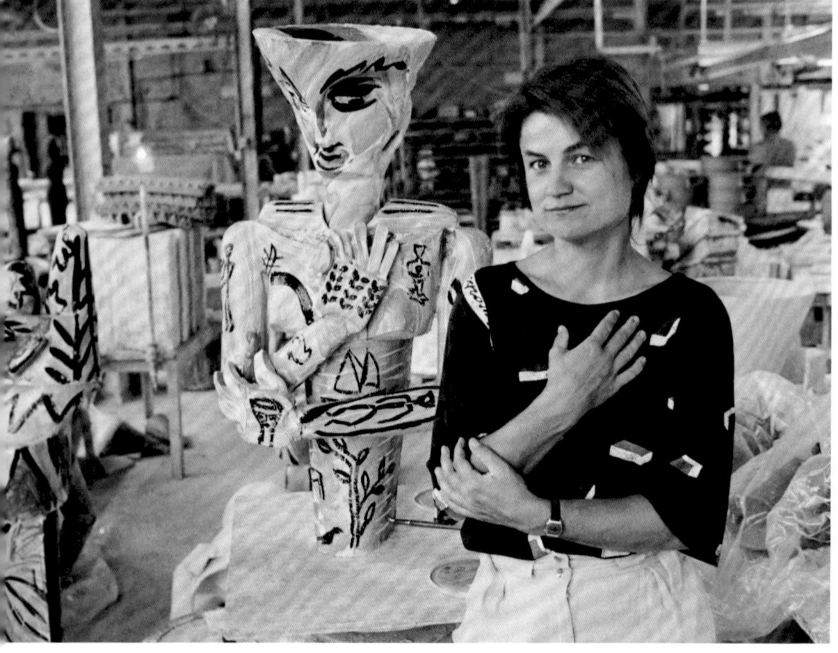

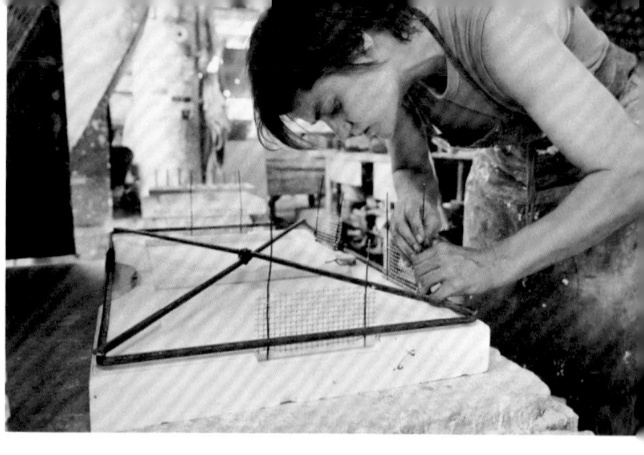

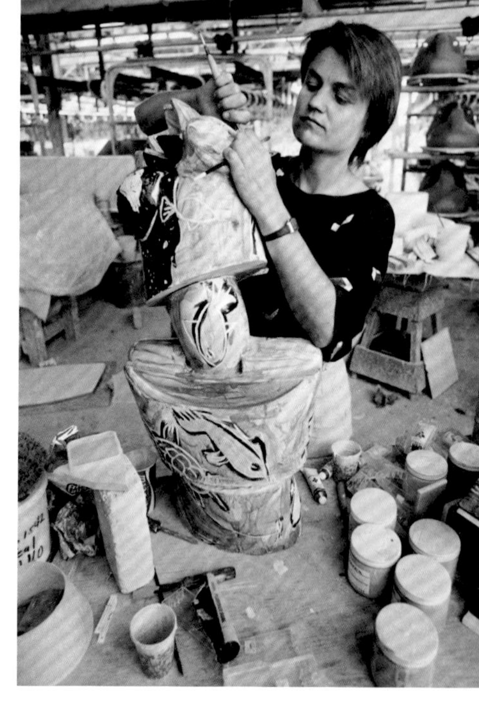

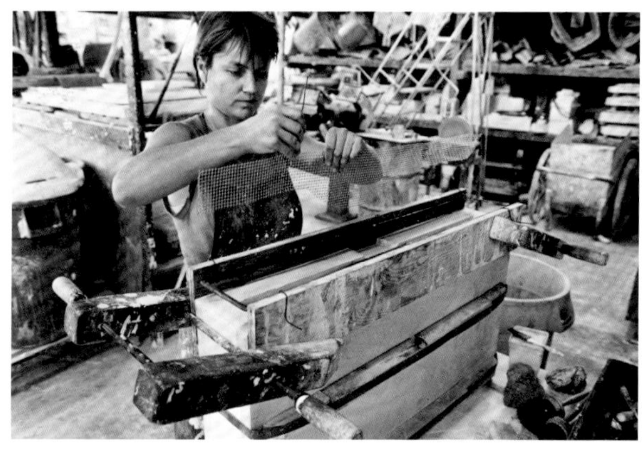

Above left
The artist's studio at Kohler Company, Kohler, Wisconsin, 1986

Above right
Block- and case-making at Kohler Company

Below left
Block- and case-making at Kohler Company
Advanced mold-making techniques learned during the Kohler residency have since been used in the artist's work.

Below right
Touching up the surface of SUMMER SAGA in the artist's studio at Kohler Company

I finally got my work to my cousin's. She had a small apartment and didn't have room to store all the boxes. In fact, she didn't even have room in her car to get them home. By the time she sent them to me, every single one of them was broken. I glued them together and painted them. They're still some of my favorite pieces.

Frey You were chosen to work at the Kohler Arts Center. What was the program there like?

PLUMMER It's an ongoing program called Arts/Industry at the Kohler Company and the John Michael Kohler Arts Center. Actually the Kohler Company and the Kohler Arts Center are two separate organizations. The company is family-owned: they say it's the biggest family-owned company left in the United States. A brother and sister still own it. The city of Sheboygan organized the Kohler Arts Center and bought the former Kohler family house for it; the Arts Center has an independent board of directors. They initiated and cosponsor this Arts/Industry program at the Kohler Company that is pretty unusual. There aren't too many companies in the U.S. where artists come in and actually work using the technology of the company.

Frey What was it like working in the factory?

PLUMMER Working at Kohler was an incredible experience. There was a huge, open studio. It went back so far you couldn't really see the end of the room and it was full of what looked like huge naked men. It turned out that they were just naked from the waist up. The molds on their work benches obscured their pants, creating the illusion of nudity. Every time I walked into the factory I felt as if I was going into a men's locker room. It was a bit of a jolt every day. However, it was a great experience to be there because of the technology available to me. I spent a lot of time up in the mold-making department. One man was assigned to help the artists with their molds. He really taught me a lot about the techniques of mold making. It got me thinking about that kind of technology in a different way.

The kilns are a hundred yards long, a football field long. That's a long kiln. You load your stuff up on these little cars, and it goes through slowly on a moving belt; it's really a little train. They'd let us use certain cars on the train and we'd load them up. A day and a half later it would come out the other end and your things would be fired.

The slip for slip casting comes out of hoses from this big overhead system. It's like the hose you use to fill your car with gasoline. Just by pressing the lever you have gallons and gallons of slip to use in your molds. Everything there is on a big scale. The cart you use to move your work around weighs two hundred pounds. Everything is far away. They have all the facilities you need, but it would literally take me about fifteen minutes to walk from the mold shop to the wood shop.

I was there for about three months and did a lot less work than I had originally planned to do. I made molds bigger than I had ever made and pieces bigger than I had made. I used some of their glazes and some of my own colors — I was able to use my own palette. I think that the forms that I used were a

Kohler Company employee

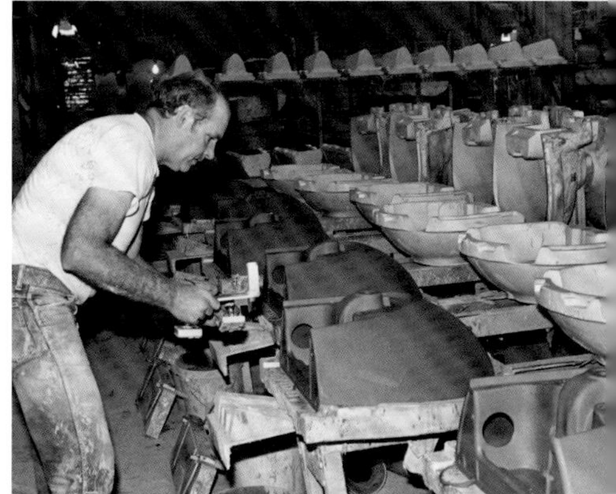

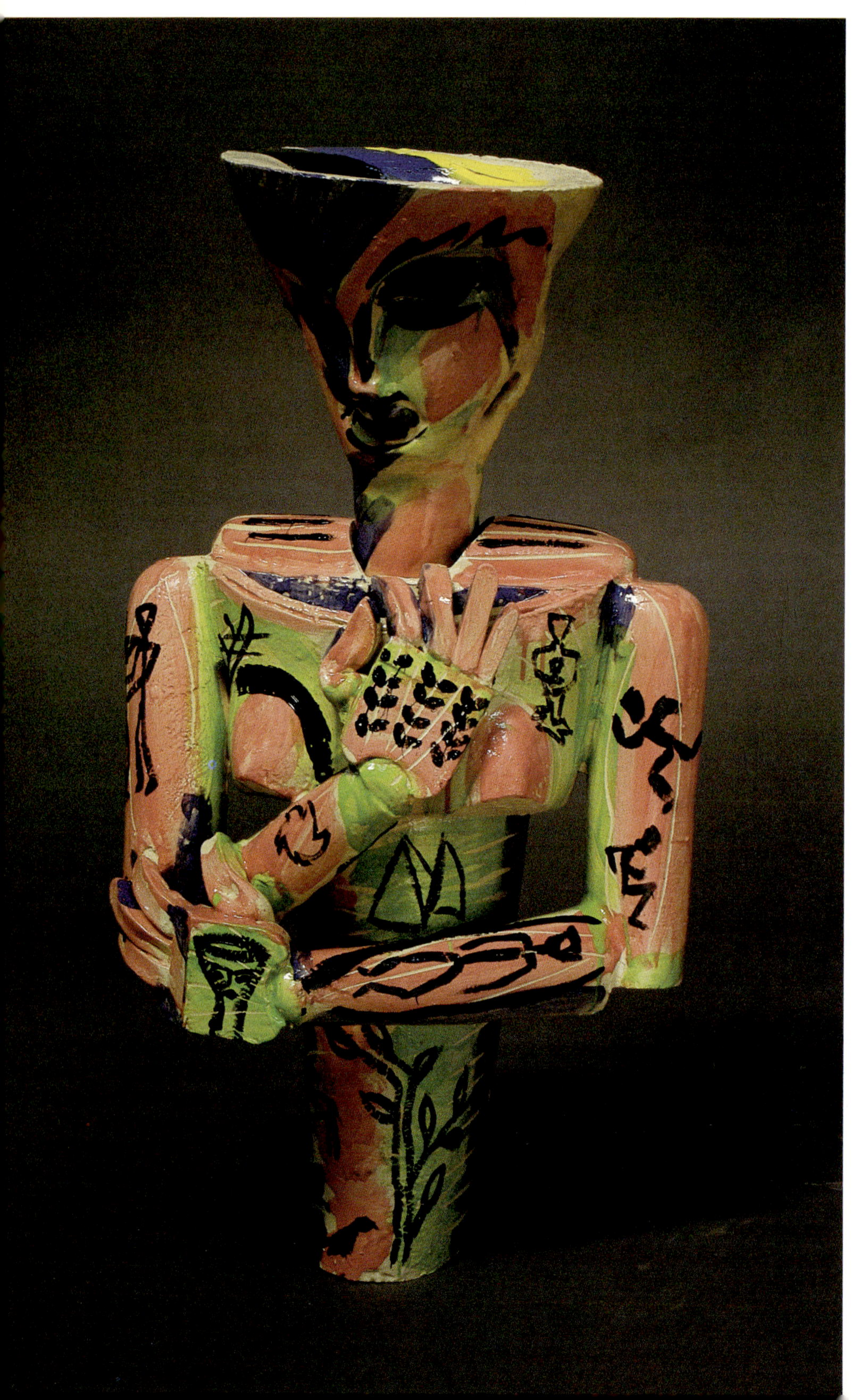

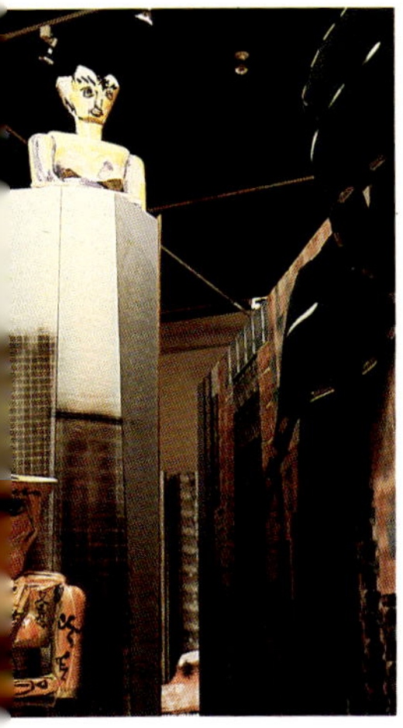

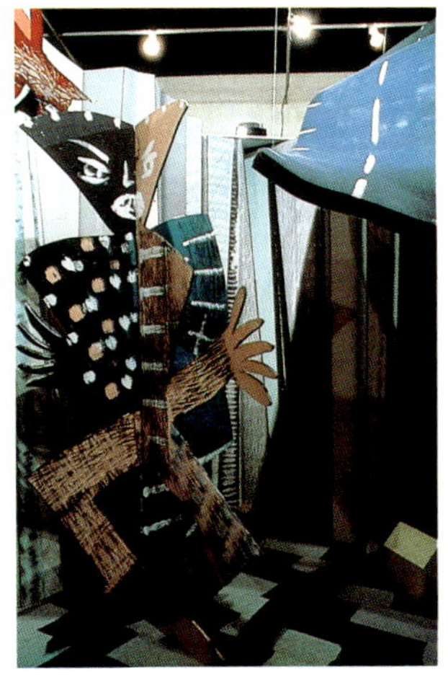

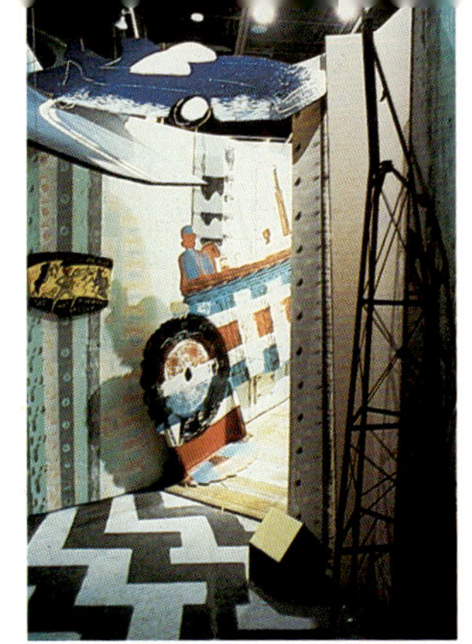

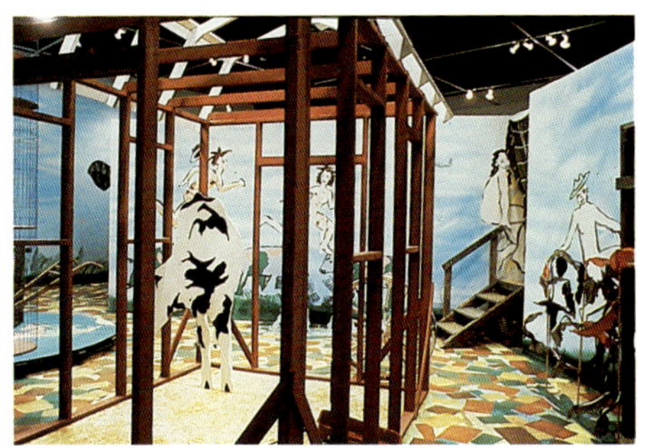

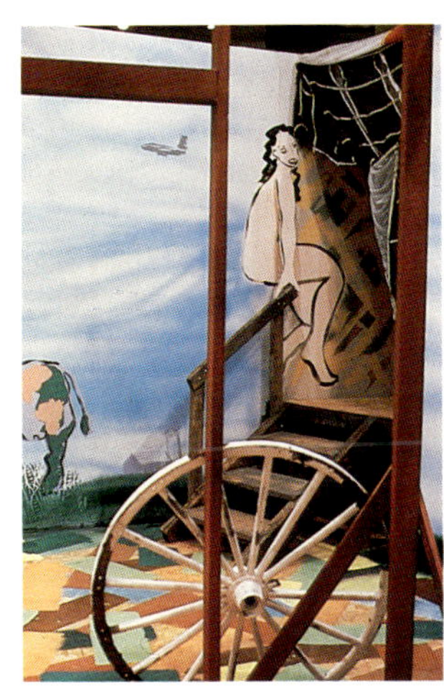

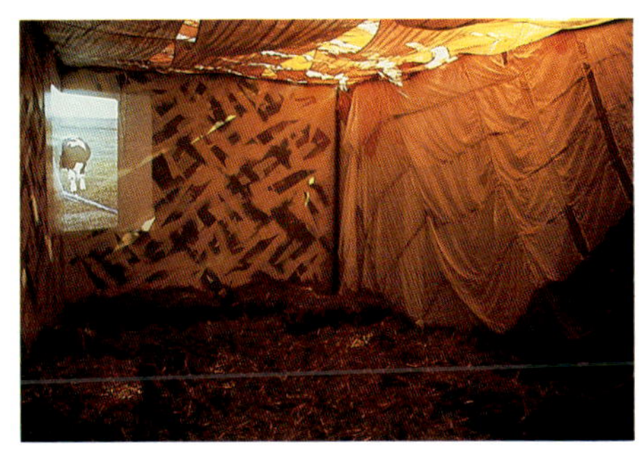

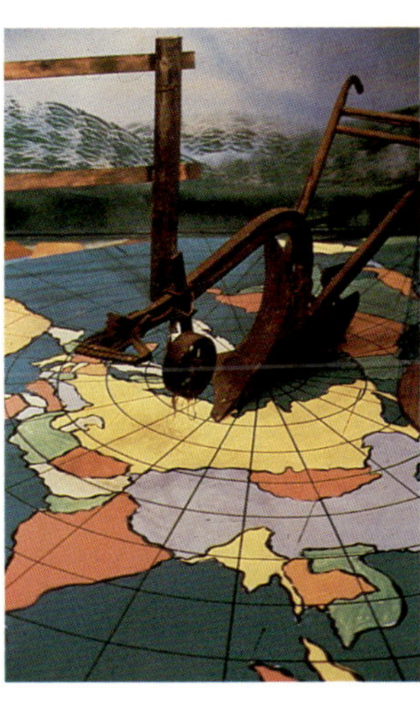

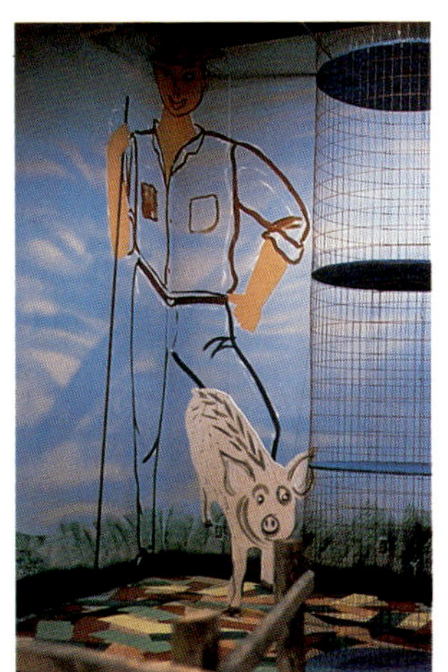

Opposite
INDUSTRY, 1986
Low-fired vitreous china
with glazes
37 x 18 x 14 in.
Made at Kohler Company
Above
FASTLANE TRACTOR, 1986
Multi-media environmen-
tal installation at John
Michael Kohler Arts
Center, Sheboygan,
Wisconsin
Gallery, 60 x 40 ft.
The viewer was led
through a section of city
out into an expanse of the
country.

little more rigid than I had in mind. As it turned out, I wasn't able to manipulate the clay because it was so non-plastic.

Since then I have used the knowledge of mold-making I gained and it has had a profound effect on my work. Before that time I wouldn't consider making, say, twenty molds in order to produce a body of work, it seemed like too much work. Since the experience at Kohler I have been able to do that.

The biggest of the pieces I made there is *Industry,* so titled because of all the kinds of work involved in making it. It wasn't a summer vacation; it really felt like a summer of hard labor, but at the same time it was work that I loved. This piece kind of represents that. There is a sink pedestal that is part of the torso of the piece. The factory workers made that element. I made the remaining nine elements by modeling original forms, making molds, casting in those molds, and finally assembling all these cast pieces — including the sink pedestal — to make the sculptural form. Later I glazed it.

At the end of my residency, they had some scheduling problems at the Arts Center. An artist who was supposed to do an installation couldn't. They had seen slides of my installation work at the LACE exhibit and asked me if I wanted to do a proposal for an installation in their main gallery for the following month, so in just a few days I put a cardboard model together. Then the job was to blow it up in 10 days to 40 by 60 feet for the gallery space.

For my subject matter I used my experience of living in Kohler, of being in the country. I have always dreamed of living in the country, having a garden, being out by the woods in nature. I contrasted my impressions of city and country living in this installation. At Kohler I was in the country, but it wasn't what I expected at all. The people around Kohler just talked about their motorcycles, beer and brauts. It was not the pastoral life that I fantasized when I thought of country living.

I was happy with the *Fastlane Tractor* installation, and kids loved running around in it. Overall you really got a sense of moving through time and space, changing environments, different things happening. It kept your attention…

Frey It looks like it was a very successful installation piece.

PLUMMER It resulted in a lot of breakthroughs for me: the use of different materials, the large scale required and the integration of kinetic and audio elements with the visual nature of my work. The installation was built to compel viewers to experience the space in different sensory ways as they moved through the different environments. I used projected images, music and sound effects to enhance all the environments. There was a silo mounted on a world that slowly turned, a flat world platform. It was the kind of thing that kids ran and jumped on. There was a hay loft with real hay that you climbed stairs to get to. There was even a section with a swing that kids would swing on.

One of the things that was really fun was that there was a limited budget for materials but there were the resources of the community. Because it was a small community we could call up so-and-so, who would say, "Oh yeah, there

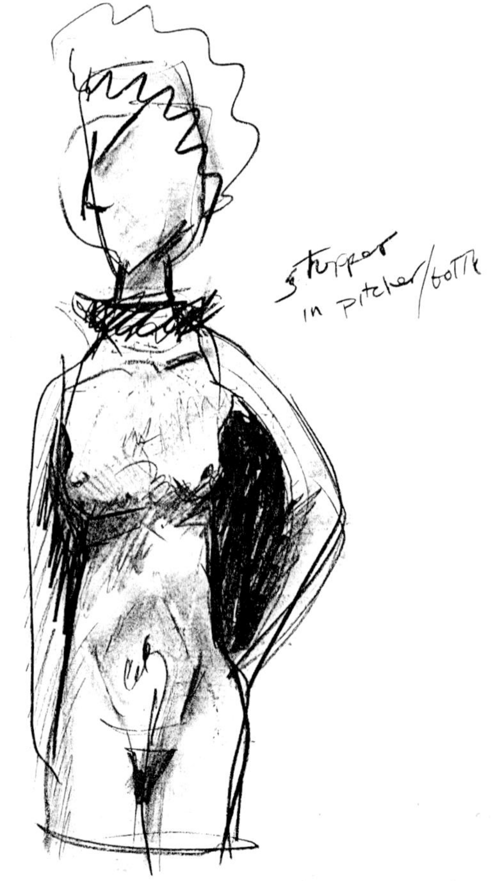

From a sketchbook, 1981

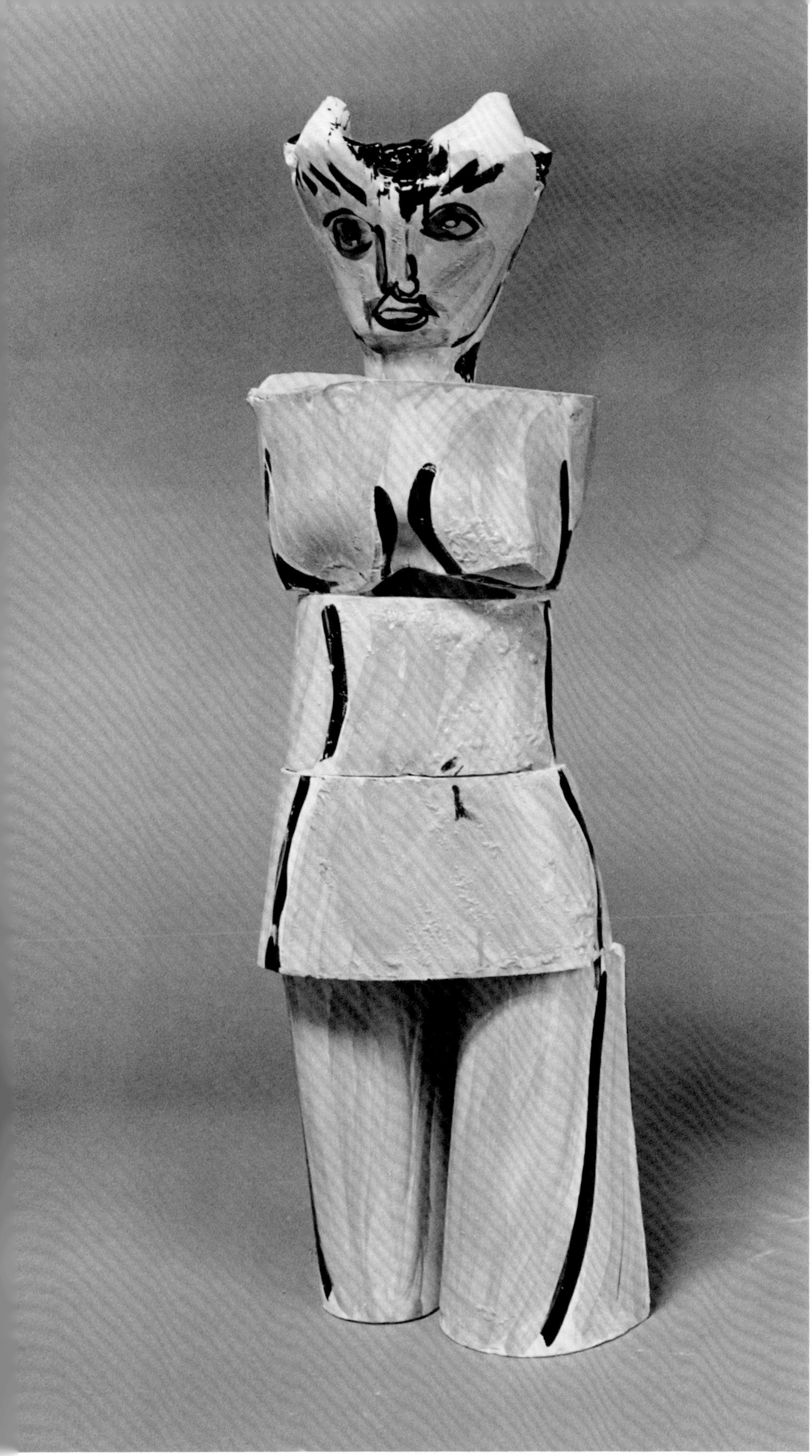

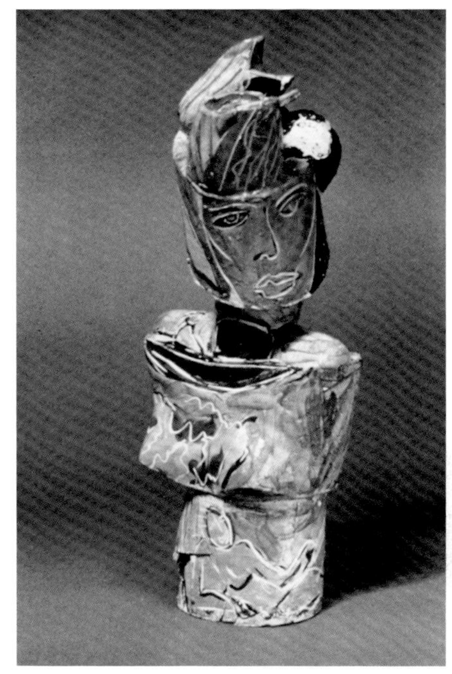

Above
SUMMER SAGA, 1986
Low-fired vitreous china
with glazes
29 x 20 x 16 in.
Made at Kohler Company
Left
VENUS DE KOHLER, 1986
Low-fired vitreous china
with glazes
47 x 13 x 12 in.
Made at Kohler Company

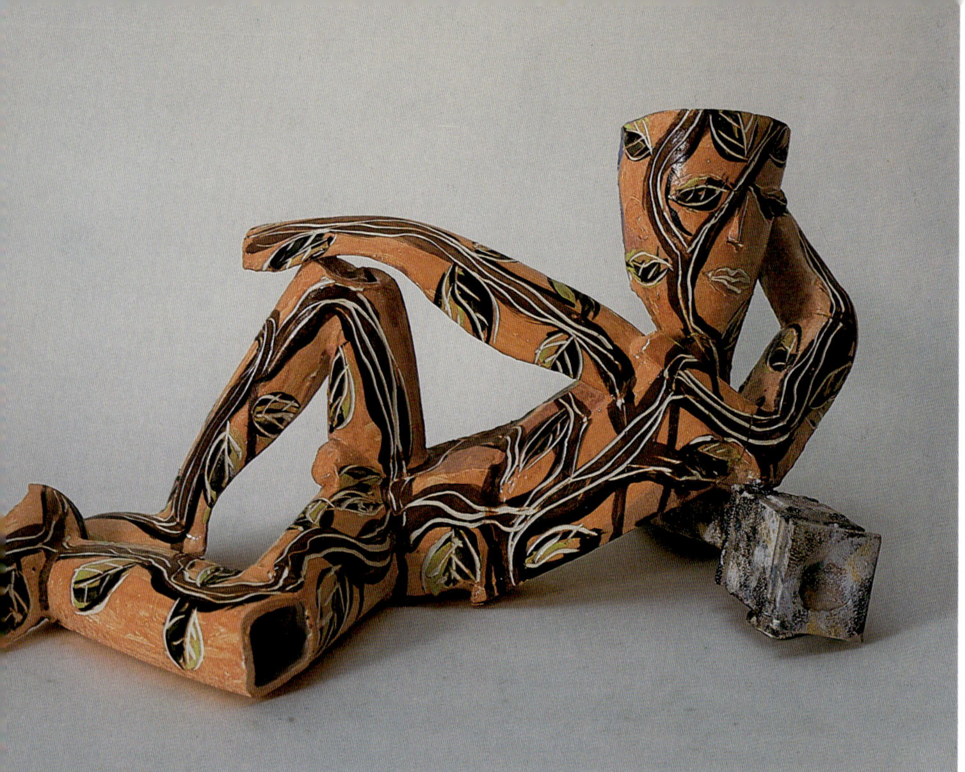

Above
Jungle Boy, 1987
Low-fire ceramic with
glazes
23 x 14 x 11 in.
Made at Lakeside Studio,
Lakeside, Michigan
Right
Garden, 1987
Acrylic on handmade
paper
22 x 30 in.

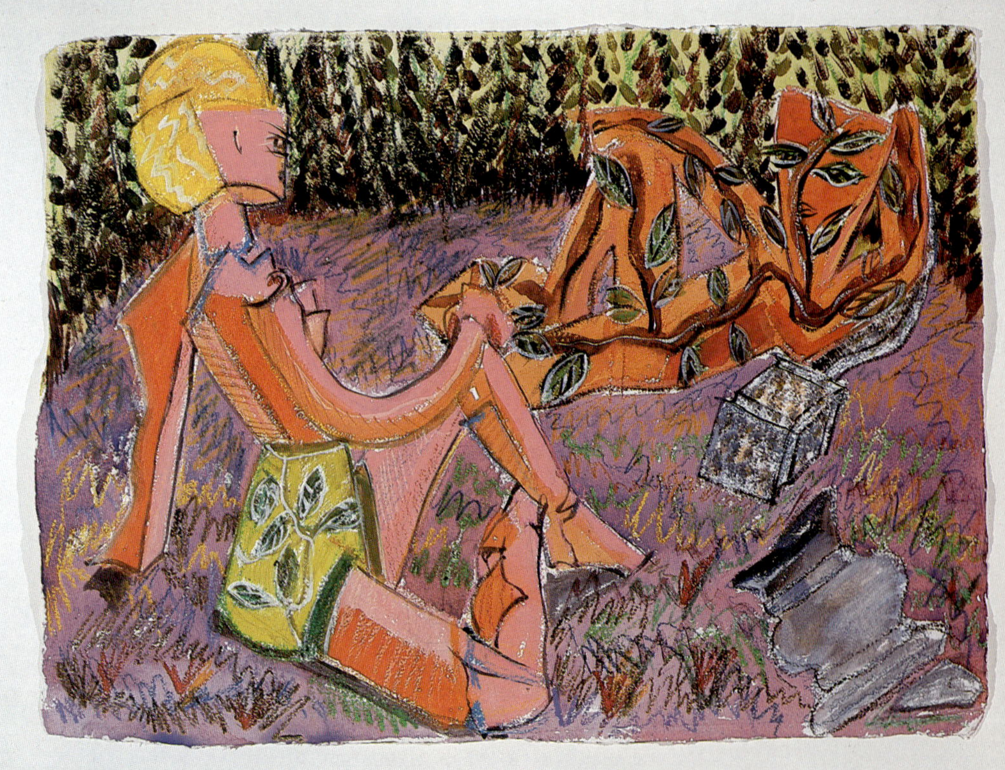

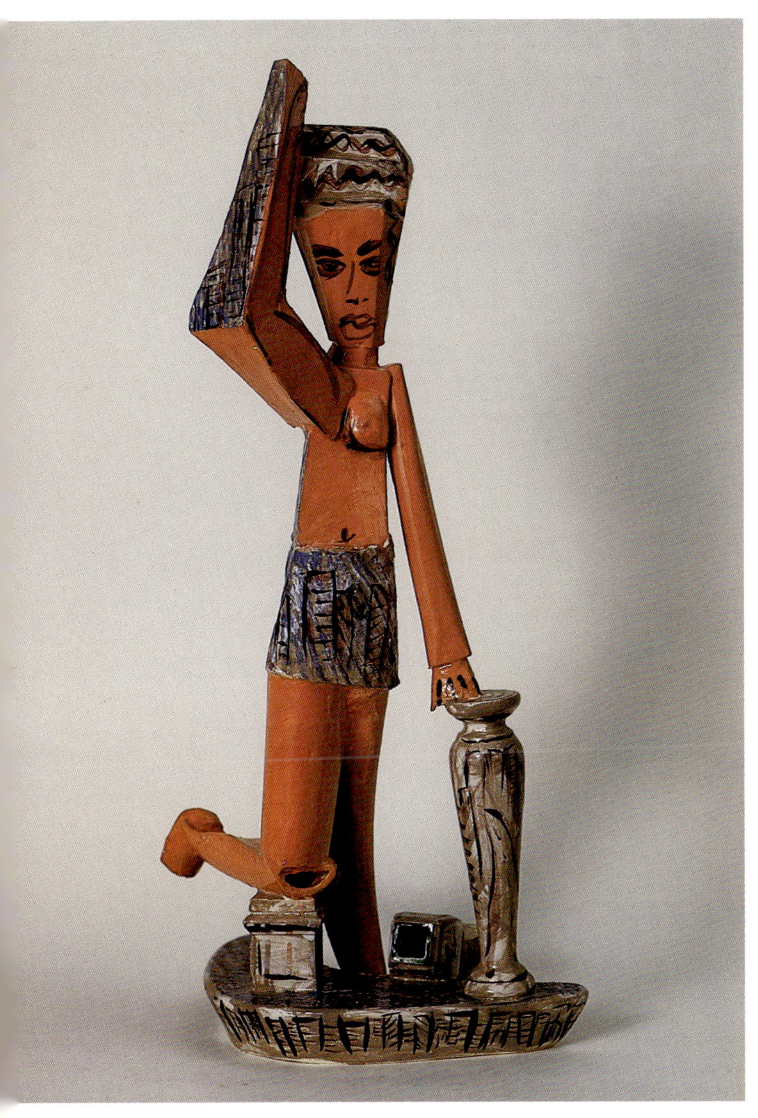

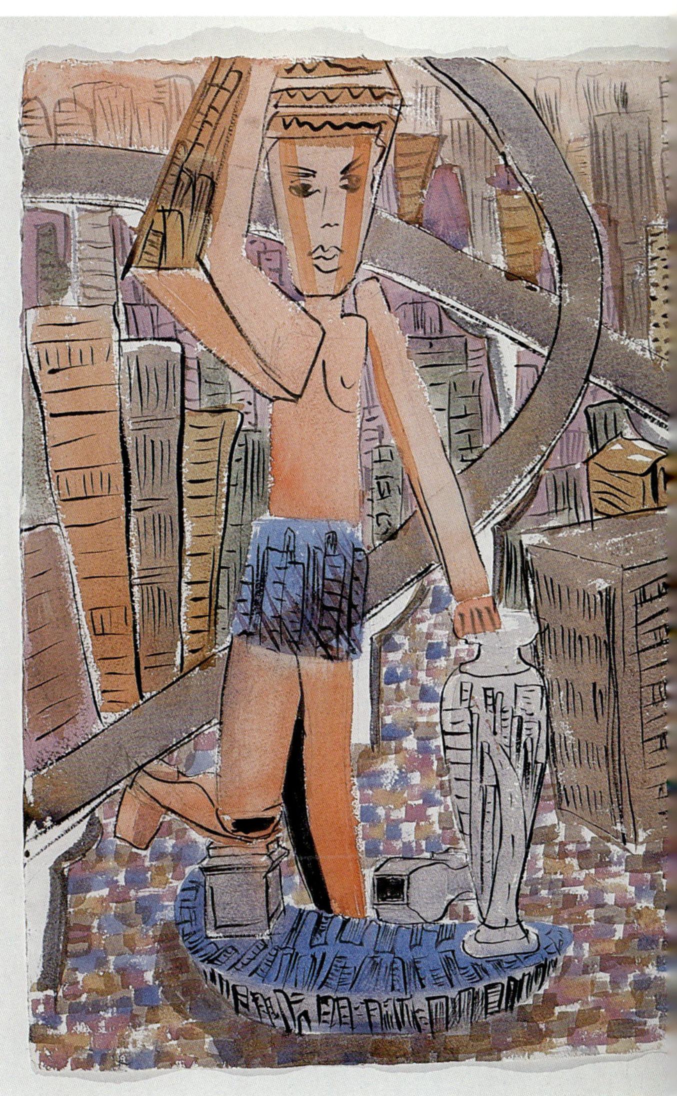

Above
CITY WOMAN, 1987
Acrylic on handmade
paper
30 x 22 in.
Left
CITY WOMAN, 1987
Low-fire ceramic with
glazes
32 x 16 x 15 in.
Made at Lakeside Studio,
Lakeside, Michigan

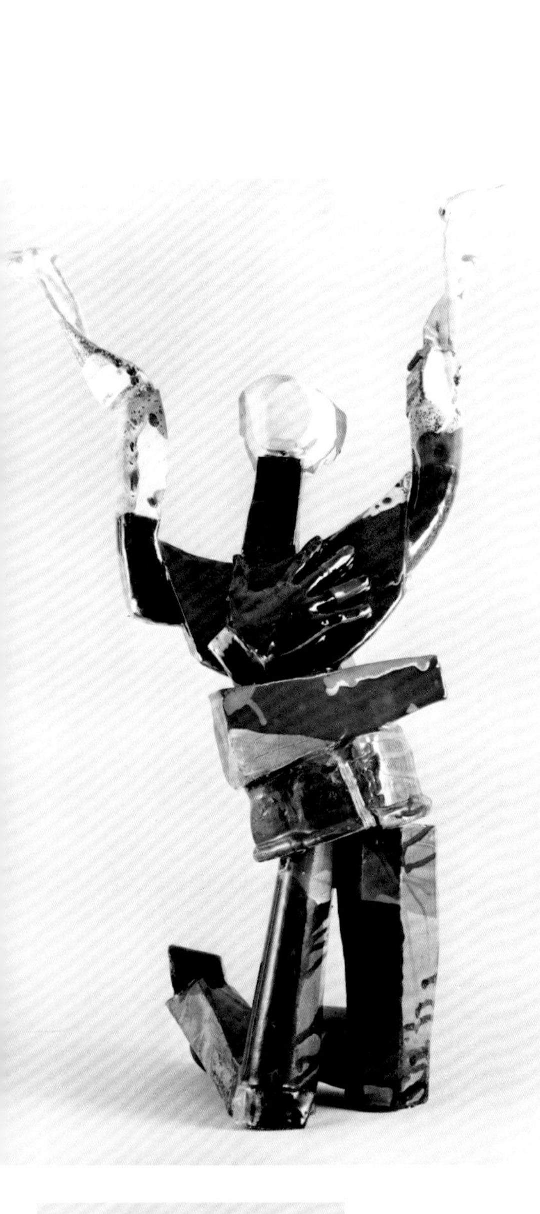

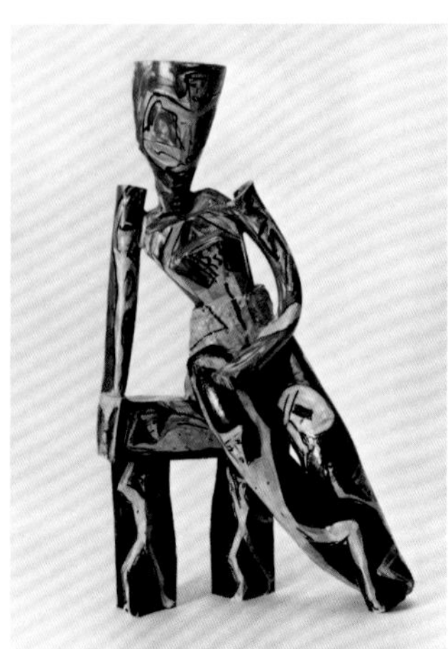

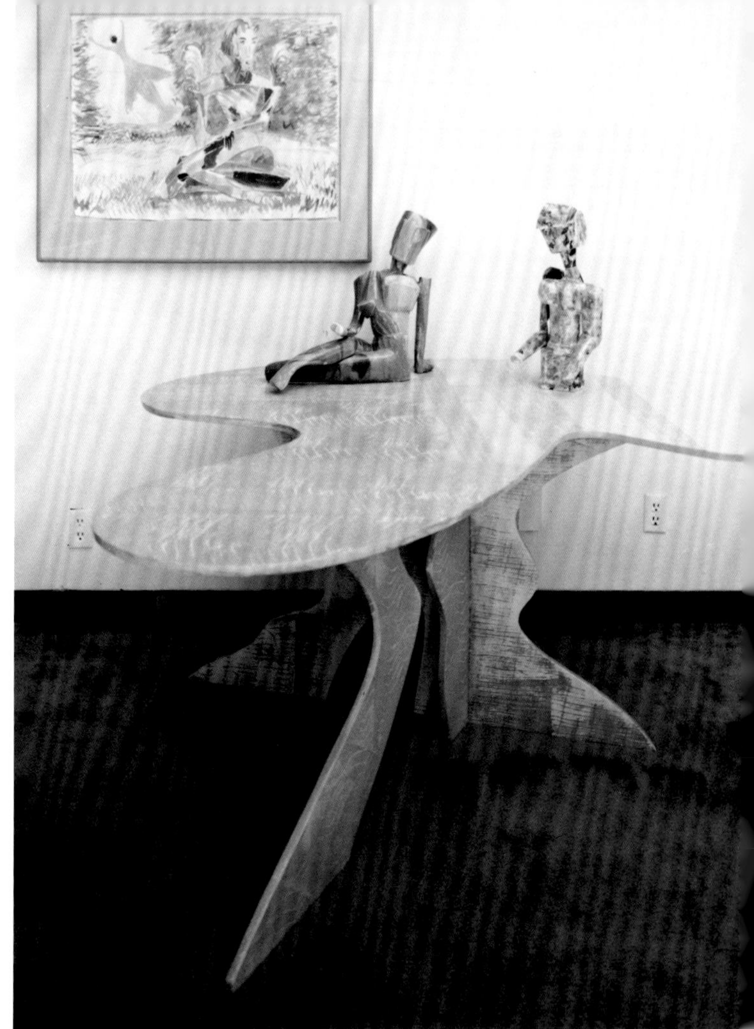

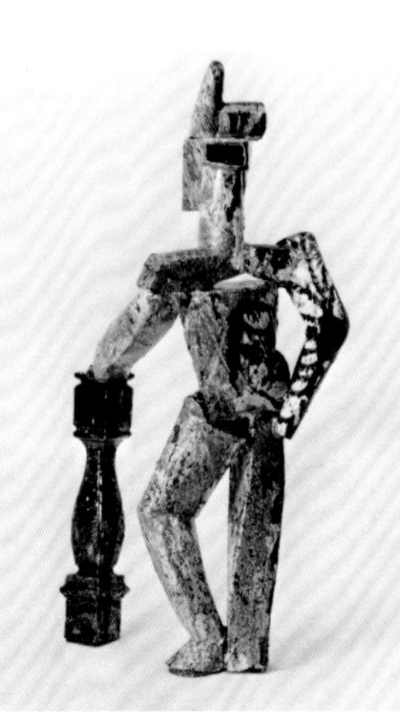

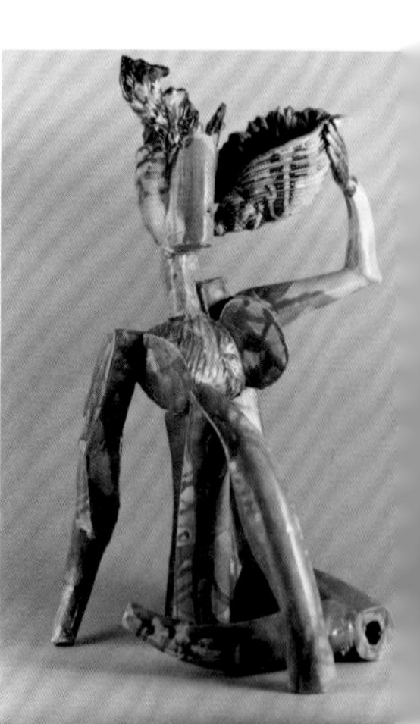

are some old plows up there; you could use one of those." Those kinds of things were available.

Frey Have you done any other installations since that experience at Kohler?

PLUMMER Yes, *La Dona Mobilé,* in the spring of 1987. It was outside in Los Angeles. It was constructed out of wood and about twenty-two feet high.

Frey Earthquake proof?

PLUMMER It was pretty solid. Someone could have run into it with a car. We had eight or ten people on it when we were installing it. I brought it over in a big truck in sections. It was inch-and-a-half plywood, and it was over-built. It weighed a ton.

It was at an intersection and was really appropriate for the site. I love the image of a modern centaur: half-woman and half-car rather than half-horse. People were always backed up in traffic right there, and so there was this idea of flying off out of the traffic. Something that I really feel in Los Angeles more than any place else that I've lived is being part of my car or my car being part of me. Of being intimately involved with the vehicle, much more than I should be.

Frey That's one of the reasons I moved from San Francisco to Oakland: it took me two hours a day to commute by public transportation. I figured that was months out of every year.

PLUMMER I proposed doing a similar piece at the San Francisco Airport: half-woman/half-airplane kind of taking off.

Frey So what do you feel your subject matter is?

PLUMMER Well, subject matter…people make differentiations between theme and subject matter, or do they? Are you making that differentiation?

Frey I think every artist has his or her subject matter, then there are many themes within that. And for an artist it's always a search; for instance, someone might describe my subject matter as going from abstraction to realism. Or from realism to abstraction. I just feel that all artists are moving. They have to move. "Move" is the operative word — such as moving from a personal to a public sense. All that together and more is my subject matter.

PLUMMER That makes sense to me. I utilize my personal experience, but I definitely am also exploring some basic human dilemmas.

I want to communicate with the viewer first on a gut level: a psychological, emotional, spiritual, visceral level rather than in an intellectual way. That's how I respond to art. That's the kind of art that I like — the kind that immediately affects me. I think that the power of art lies in that kind of direct communication with something other than your mind, with a deeper part of yourself, a more basic part.

Primarily I address some of the dilemmas of human existence through the use of the figure. For instance, *David and Goliath,* which I did in Paris, addresses an important psychological reality that we encounter today. To me that story is about facing an insurmountable challenge, of being presented with

Opposite, above left
RAIN PRAYER, 1988
Low-fire ceramic with glazes
31 x 14 x 20 in.
Opposite, above right
Installation of domestic setting, 1988, including MODERN WINGS, 1988, acrylic on handmade paper, 22 x 30 in.; TABLE, wood and acrylic, 57 x 55 x 31 in.; DANCER, 1988, low-fire ceramic with glazes, 15 x 6 x 9 in.; BATHING BEAUTY, 1988, low-fire ceramic with glazes, 10 x 17 x 8 in.
Opposite, below left
WOMAN WITH DANCERS, 1987
Low-fire ceramic with glazes
24 x 13 x 8 in.
Opposite, below middle
MAN WHO STOOD IN ONE PLACE, 1987
Low-fire ceramic with glazes
24 x 11 x 9 in.
Opposite, below right
SIREN SONG, 1988
Low-fire ceramic with glazes
26 x 14 x 12 in.

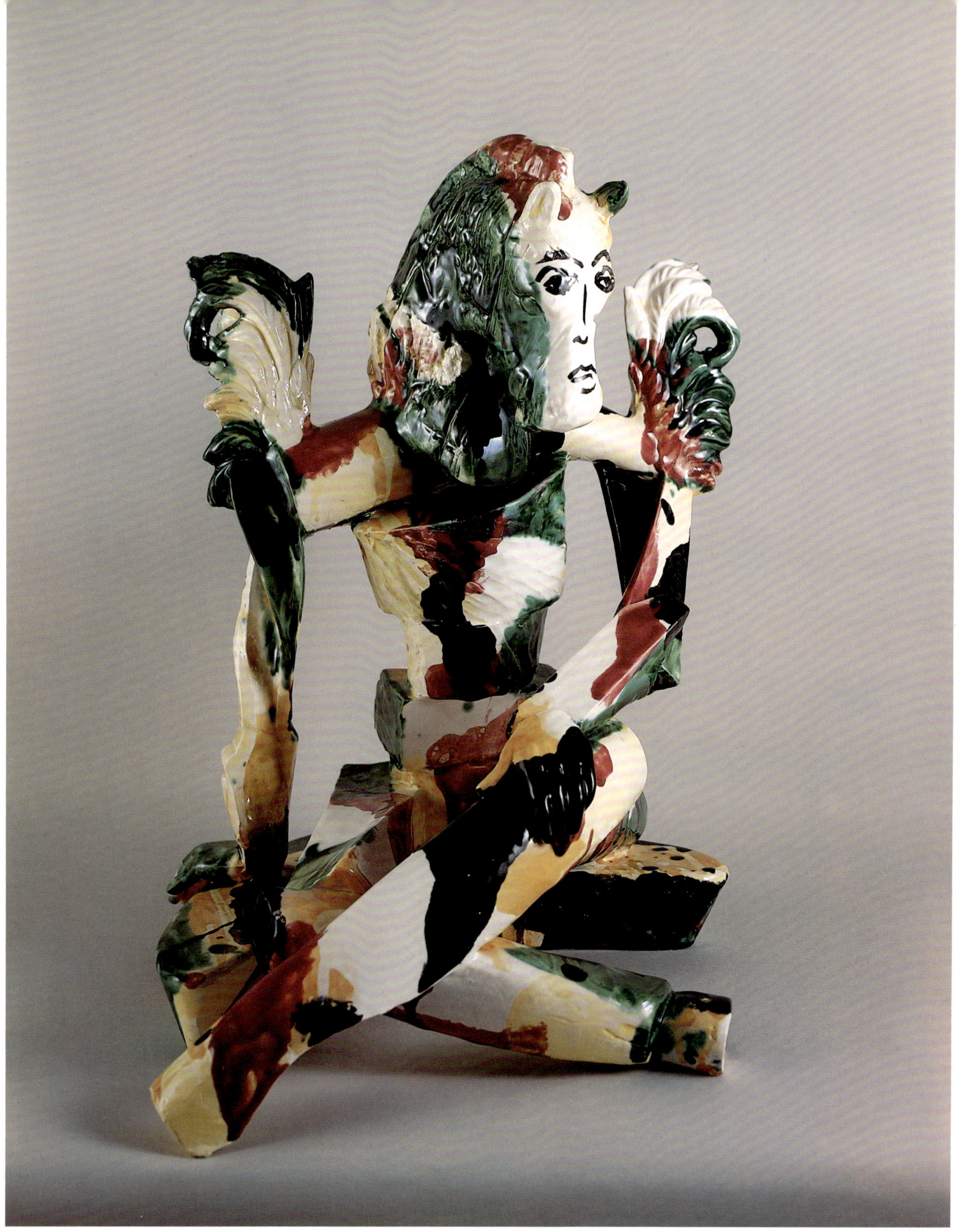

something that you cannot overcome, something that is much larger than you, something that poses a challenge at which you should fail. In the face of certain failure, you attempt to overcome the obstacle anyway. When you succeed, you experience that sense of bewilderment, relief and awe. The moment after beheading Goliath, David can hardly believe that he has succeeded and becomes aware of the help of God. He feels an inner strength of which he was previously unaware. That's the moment that I want to convey to the viewer. By using the figure I try to create that experience for a viewer with my work.

The process of making art is important for me. In fact, the creative process itself is the most important aspect of artmaking to me. The end product is gratifying, but it's no longer living art in my mind. Living art is the act of creation. I do not have a precise image of my finished piece before it is completed. I do have a basic concept and I work towards that. Shortly after I begin, the piece generally takes on a life of its own. It starts to have its own spirit, its own character and its own input. Then there's a sense of collaboration because the work is speaking back to me. I see new things through it. *Siren Song* is a good example. Before the bisque firing the image was of a seated woman blowing a conch shell as a trumpet. She was using nature to amplify her message. The bisque firing distorted the piece in such a way that she is now listening to the message from the conch shell. That is the "happy accident" that Paul Soldner talks about; he utilizes it a lot with firing. Soldner espouses leaving your technique open enough for there to be accidental results. Sometimes those accidents simply result in discarded pieces, but other times, as in *Siren Song* a "happy accident" results in a piece superior to the one you may have originally conceived.

I still puzzle over what it all means after I finish it. I don't have all the answers, and that's what keeps me excited about doing this work.

Frey In some of your early pieces you used molds of familiar objects such as roosters.

PLUMMER

I'm doing a couple of different things with them. In one way I use them as abstracted forms. Actually, a lot of people who aren't familiar with the ceramic process never see the rooster or the fish or the duck unless you point it out. They don't catch on. It's for form and texture. Sometimes in a figurative sculpture I'll use a mold as a kind of headdress, like an explosion coming out of the head, more than as a literal reference to the rooster or fish. These is also a play on the fact that these cast objects are very low art with distant origins in higher art. I'm returning them to the realm of high art in a backhanded way.

Frey This country, Japan and I think Canada are the only countries in the world where you can get these kinds of ready-made things.

PLUMMER That's good news. That means that I can go to Japan and work.

Frey It's interesting that molds are used worldwide and cross time and cultures. They go back hundreds of years and they go across all cultures.

Opposite
MASKED PEGASUS, 1988
Low-fire ceramic with
glazes
19 x 14 x 18 in.

PLUMMER Like all the Buddhas and traditional Chinese vases...

Frey And Greek vases and Walt Disney.

PLUMMER Things that are from the 18th and 19th century.

Frey They're all there. I think I read once that in order for them to continue production of those figurines they have to sell at a rate of about 100,000 a year — for the image to become popular enough to continue. Why are people still buying 18th-century Meissen figurine groups, or even worse?

PLUMMER Because they're familiar and they want art, they want decoration. They can understand them, and little ceramic things are so intimate. You can pick them up and they're nice to touch. They're more comforting in a way than something you put up on the wall. Not everyone wants to be challenged by their home environment. They feel challenged enough by the environment outside. They want to be comforted at home, so they surround themselves with these little familiar things that make them feel good.

Frey That certainly is part of it...if you think of the 18th- and 19th-century figurine groups, the farmers were depicted as being happy, even with patches on their clothes. That was to make poverty and hunger less of a threat. To take the tigers and panthers and make them also into less of a threat. Comfort is one of the reasons people look at art or even want art.

PLUMMER I think artists and people seriously involved want art that is challenging, but the vast majority of people want comfort, reaffirmation. They want art to make them feel good about themselves and don't want art to be difficult, challenging or to show the dark side.

Frey Well, what are you working on now?

PLUMMER On pieces that relate to the ideas I was exploring in Paris. Those pieces were very small and unglazed. The new work is larger, more complex, and involves a wider range of images. The pieces incorporate my own forms as well as found forms from molds. Also, I was just commissioned to make a sculptural fountain for a courtyard in a restored fifties apartment building in the Hollywood redevelopment area. It's a lot of work, but I am excited about having an outdoor piece that utilizes the dynamics of moving water. I also want to enlarge my figures to monumental scale and include more narrative elements, such as the environment and multiple characters.

Just when I think I know what I am going to do next, a new project presents itself and my work changes direction.

Chronology

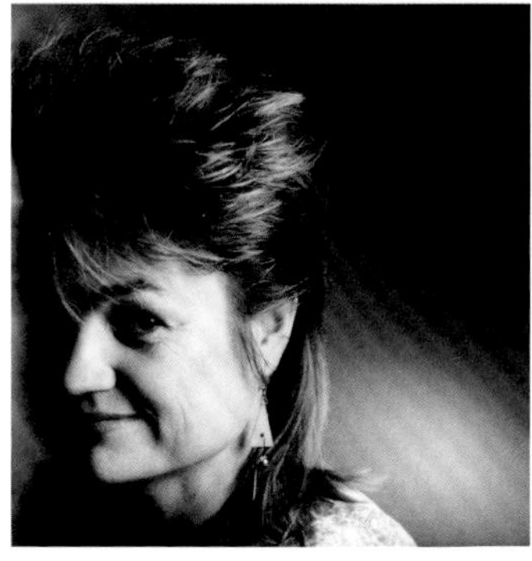

Anne Scott Plummer
Portrait by Bonnie Shiffman
1988

1951
Born in Providence, Rhode Island.

1966
Creates ceramic head/vessel with related drawing.

1968
Makes polychrome figurative sculpture.

1969
Joins U.S. Air Force, is trained and works as air traffic controller. Stationed in Biloxi, Mississippi, and Hampton, Virginia. Lampoons military life in cartoons; begins painting dream imagery.

1971
Receives honorable discharge from Air Force; travels throughout U.S. in Volkswagen van, painting and photographing.

1972–75
Joins Provincetown (Mass.) Art Association, exhibits impressionist paintings. Learns pottery from Harry Holl in Dennis, Massachusetts, and at Clayworks in Provincetown.

1975–79
Studies ceramics, sculpture and drawing at Rhode Island School of Design, Providence, Rhode Island, studying with, among others, Jacqueline Rice and John Gill. Earns academic honors, 1976. Works at Spring Pottery, Newport, R.I., during summers. Is graduated with B.F.A. in 1979. Creates "Lady in Black" series of plates.

1979
In fall begins studying ceramic sculpture in M.F.A. program at Claremont Graduate School, Claremont, California, with Paul Soldner. Produces "East Coast Cowgirl" series of large vessels.

1980
Graduate teaching fellow in sculpture. During summer studies at Sun Valley Center of Arts and Humanities, Sun Valley, Idaho; creates "Oribe Cowgirl" low vessels. Is studio assistant for Los Angeles painter Tom Wudl.

1981
Is graduated from Claremont with M.F.A. in ceramic sculpture. Begins teaching at University of Southern California, Los Angeles. Takes studio in downtown Los Angeles. Has solo exhibition titled "Axact" in entrance gallery of Los Angeles Institute of Contemporary Art.

1983–84
Is artist-in-residence at Sun Valley Center of Arts and Humanities during summers. Makes "Kiln" series of sculptures. Awarded gold medal in "Ninth International Biennale of Ceramic Art," Vallauris, France.

1985
Travels in Europe for four months; works at Atelier Jeanclous, Ecole Nationale Supérieure des Beaux-Arts, Paris, and creates figurative sculptures based on myths. Is studio assistant for Los Angeles sculptor Mark Lere.

1986
Assists on archaeological dig in Sarteneja, Belize, discovering, sketching and identifying bones and discovering and repairing pottery from A.D. 1100 Mayan burial site.
Is artist-in-residence at Kohler Company, Kohler, Wisconsin, in Arts/Industry Program of John Michael Kohler Arts Center, Sheboygan, Wis. Makes life-sized figurative sculptures; creates *Fastlane Tractor* multi-media installation at Kohler Arts Center.

1987
Installs monumental sculpture *La Dona Mobilé* in West Hollywood, California, for "Art on the Island" project.
As artist-in-residence at Lakeside Studio, Lakeside, Michigan, produces figurative sculptures with related drawings.

1988
Receives commission for sculptural fountain for courtyard of apartment building, Hollywood, California.

Myth in Clay Form

MARTHA DREXLER LYNN

Anne Scott Plummer's sculpture exemplifies the potential and the freedom now accorded to clay art of the late twentieth century. It also partakes of the postmodernist feast of multicultural, multilayered references and sensibilities. Unlike many artists who began as potters, Plummer has always seen herself as an artist/painter/sculptor. She wrestles only with finding the correct mix of expressive elements with which to work. While having chosen clay as her primary medium, this sureness of artistic identity gives her the confidence to combine a number of seemingly disparate materials, scales and motifs. She fashions gestural figures and amplifies them with painterly glazes, achieving a synthesis that conveys both charm and power through the human form.

In order to understand the uniqueness of her work and its place, several basics need to be reviewed. Clay as a medium is the embodiment of form, with glaze or paint adding the color and decoration, the articulation and immediate communication. Clay in the 1980s has benefited from the strides made during the rebellious years since 1952. In the late seventies clay emerged from its earlier associations with the crafts and function and became free to address any formal issue and to express content previously reserved only for the traditionally sanctified media. Clay now stands at the meeting point of ceramic tradition and art. Plummer uses all of these potentials to explore various scales (from several inches to over twenty feet) and clay techniques (coil built, thrown, cast, modeled) as well as the mixing of media. All are used to create pieces that reflect her response to life and her interest in questions both big and small. As a product of the elevation of clay and the evaporation of the lines between the fine arts and the crafts-based arts, Plummer codifies these to create her evocative vessel cum sculptural pieces.

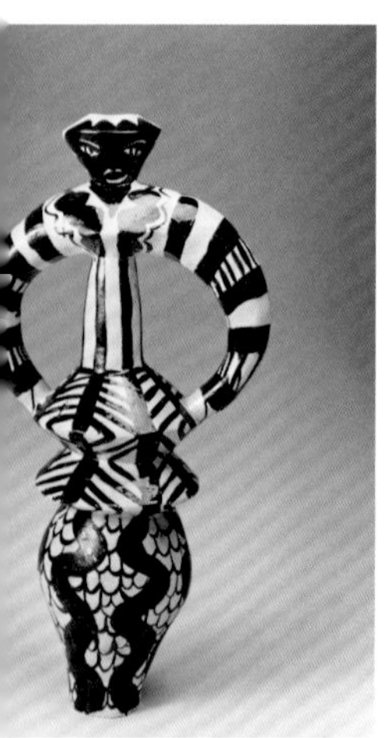

PETER HUNT'S AFRICA, 1988
Low-fire ceramic with glazes
38 x 20 x 16 in.

But Plummer is most drawn to the sculptural and figurative potential of clay. True to her artist's rather than a potter's orientation, the human aspect, in both content and formal reference, has assumed the primary position. True to her time and her training under process- and value-oriented Paul Soldner and intellectual, conceptual Roland Reiss, her figures are gestural. Movement conveys content. This can be seen in the receptive hand gesture of *Saxophone Muse*, 1985 (page 11), and hipshot pose of *Inès*, 1988 (page 2). Such quick takes cut to the heart of these pieces' intent. The impact comes from Plummer's adroit use of this shorthand communication. Her work is also informed by a knowledge of ceramic precedents. Her figures are often formally constructed with vessel-like heads and conical limbs; her figure-size vessels also resonate with the echoes of ceramics' figurative history, at once being archaic and constructivist.

Plummer's development has been furthered by her traveling and working in various parts of the United States and France. Her diverse experiences prompted larger questions about human life while she honed her technique and formal vocabulary, as well as her use of humor. This can be seen by tracing the progress of her artistic output.

Six of Plummer's works were exhibited in *Earth and Fire: The Marer Collection of Contemporary Ceramics* at the Montgomery Gallery of Pomona College, Claremont, California, in 1984. Two were vessels and four were figural/sculptural. One of the latter was *Circus*, 1980 (page 9), and in it are elements that remain constants in her work. Fashioned out of low-fire clay and acrylic paint, the piece is formally gestural. Seemingly random, almost found bits of clay coalesce into a figure caught in suspended motion. Through the casually modeled clay she succeeds in capturing the essence of a circus performer in action. This quick clay jotting combines two potent qualities of her art: whimsy and movement.

VOC, 1982, is a bust placed on top of a table form that by implication becomes its body. It too is economical in detail and constructivist in content, but here another element is added: mixed media. While clay is still used for the head, the supporting structure/body is made of wood and formica. Such a juxtaposition allows the artist to wrestle with the dualities inherent in combined mate-

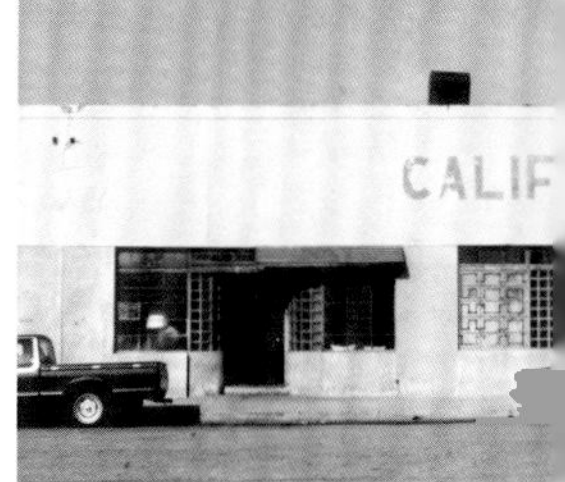

The artist's Boyd Street studio
(1981–84), Los Angeles

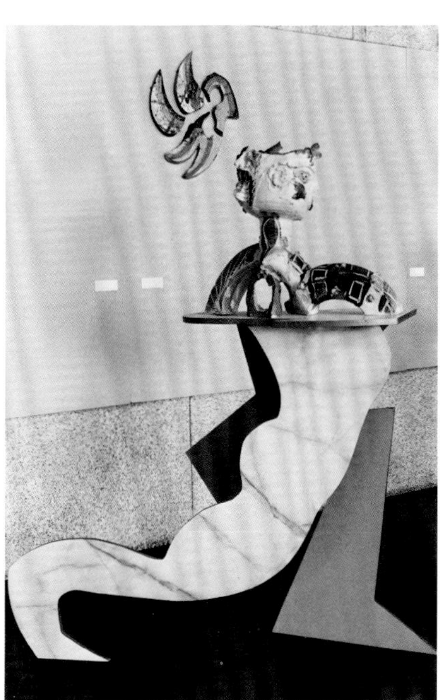

VOC, 1982
Ceramic with glazes, wood
and plastic laminate
70 x 30 x 35 in.

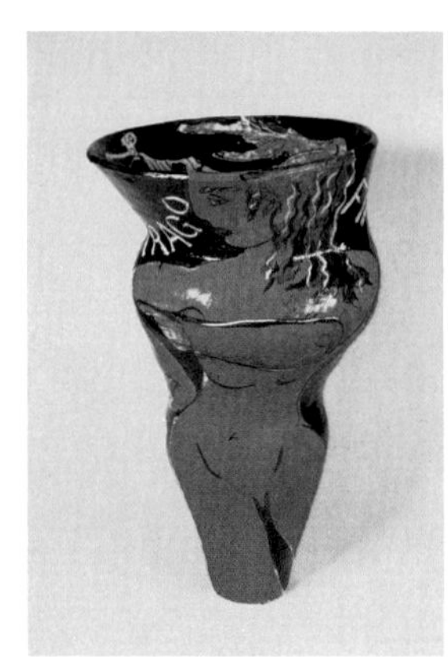

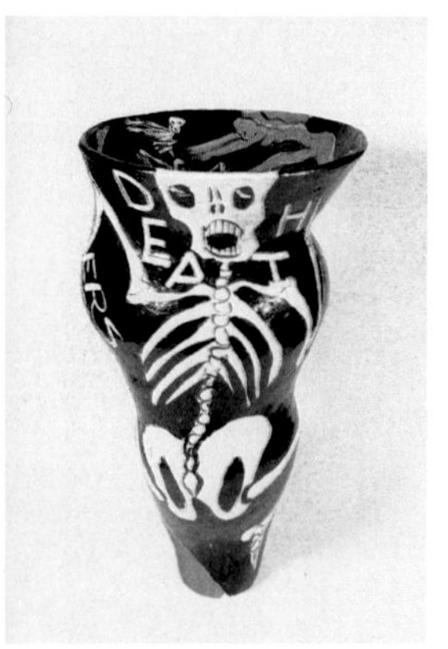

VIRAGO FINGERS DEATH, 1986
Low-fire ceramic with
glazes
39 x 20 x 16 in.

rials and forms. Plummer is fascinated by such dualities and their incipient resolution, which results in what she calls "true aesthetic harmony." This melding of the intuitive and the rational is a central theme in her work.

In 1986, while on a Arts/Industry residency at the Kohler Company, manufacturers of sanitary ceramics, Plummer created for the John Michael Kohler Arts Center her third installation piece, a multimedia *tour de force* exploring conflicting images of the city and the countryside. Focusing on a generic urban environment and using a maze-like tangle of building facades, *Fastlane Tractor* (page 17) incorporated such materials as wood, foam, fabric, hay, paint and projected slides to explore the intersection of urban and rural. The contrasts were many — visual, olfactory and spatial — and they again dealt with notions of inevitable and irreconcilable dualities. In this environment she placed her constructivist, gestural busts, including *Industry* (page 16) and *Summer Saga* (page 19). These titles, while carrying a hint of satire, also reveal the artist's interest in the use of personification. As her work has matured, Plummer has come to delight in communicating abstract concepts through figuration.

This artistic approach was fully developed in her outdoor monumental sculpture *La Dona Mobilé*, 1987 (cover). Here Plummer eschewed her customary clay and worked in wood, steel and acrylic while maintaining her formal and thematic idiom. Sited on a roadway median, the piece depicted a modern-day feminized centaur/fish-headed car who energetically gesticulates toward the sky. Movement again expresses the artist's humor, and implies a willingness to charge out into the worldly fray. Painted with saturated tints, *La Dona Mobilé* created a collage of images that whimsically jostled each other for precedence. Drawing on her interest in myth, Plummer successfully melded the classical notion of the half-(wo)man and half-(car)beast — with its subtext of the centaur's personification of clouds and the sun — to the contemporary reality of the legions of women who dash around the urban scene in their workhorse chariots. One wonders if the title refers to the time-honored male notion that all women are fickle, here perhaps applied to perceived female driving patterns. It is this type of double entendre that intrigues Plummer's audience.

In her most recent figurative work Plummer returns to small scale. The gestural and assembled aspects remain, and her content has matured to include classical themes presented through a modern eye. In *Masked Pegasus*, 1988 (page 24), she presents a figure inspired by the Greek myth of Pegasus, who, like centaurs, is one of the sun cattle and also associated with clouds. Plummer reconstructs the image of the winged horse Pegasus by adding a dash of reversed centaur imagery, placing a horse-like head on a human-like body.

Plummer also continues her exploration of dualities as she wrestles with the male/female dichotomy in her interpretation of Pegasus. The classical Pegasus had the inherent tension of being born of seaform (Neptune) and the blood of Medusa, but by flipping the stereotypic images, both sexual and classical, Plummer adds a post-sixties depth. The result is a graceful figure whose face appears beseechingly female. It is interesting to speculate on the intention of the application of the glaze: casually applied, it is evocative of Pegasus' association with the ever-changing configuration of clouds.

Anne Scott Plummer enters her second decade as a ceramic sculptor with a growing repertoire of images and concepts who has developed her formal and technical strengths to match and express her content. By first being an artist, one who chooses to use clay as well as other mediums, she brings the best of all to her work. This combined with the drawing from past lore and current realities continue to inform and energize her art.

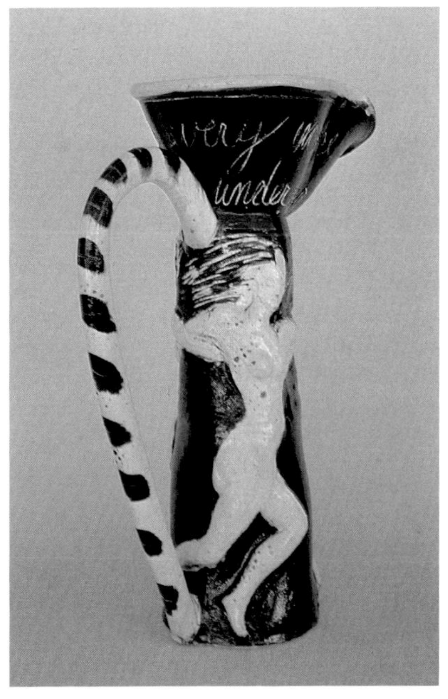

**ALTERNATING UNDERCURRENTS,
1979
Raku-fired ceramic with
glazes
36 x 15 x 10 in.**

Martha Drexler Lynn has just completed a catalogue of the Smits collection of contemporary ceramics at the Los Angeles County Museum of Art, where she is in charge developing the collection of twentieth-century decorative arts.

Exhibitions

SOLO

1989

"New Work,"
Koslow Gallery
Los Angeles, California
"Abstracted Myth," Showcase
Gallery, Cerritos College,
Norwalk, California

1988

"New Work," Koslow Rayl Fine
Art, Los Angeles

1987

"New Sculpture," Koslow Rayl
Fine Art, Los Angeles

1986

"Fastlane Tractor," multi-media
installation, John Michael Kohler
Arts Center, Sheboygan,
Wisconsin
"New Sculpture," Theater
Gallery, Design Center of
Los Angeles

1985

"Ceramic Sculpture," Base 2,
Hollywood, California
"Recent Sculptures," Sight and
Sound Gallery, California State
University at Northridge,
California

1981

"Axact," Entrance Gallery,
Los Angeles Institute of Con-
temporary Art, Los Angeles
"Bustz," Libra Gallery,
Claremont Graduate School,
Claremont, California
"Fired Punk Rock," Libra
Gallery, Claremont Graduate
School, Claremont

GROUP

1989

"Clay III"
Mount St. Mary's College,
Los Angeles
"Ceramic Bi Annual,"
Pasadena City College,
Pasadena, California
"Scripps Ceramic Annual,"
Galleries of the Claremont
Colleges, Claremont

1988

"The View From Los Angeles,"
Sawhill Gallery, James Madison
University, Harrisonburg,
Virginia
"Scripps Ceramic Annual,"
Galleries of the Claremont
Colleges, Claremont
"Figurative Art Now," East
Gallery, California State Univer-
sity, Fullerton, California
"Members' Salon," The
Woman's Building Gallery,
Los Angeles
"Miniature Golf," Casa de Rosa
Gallery, Los Angeles
CARECEN Auction to benefit
Central American Refugee
Center

1987

"Art On The Island," City of
West Hollywood, California
"New Art Forms," Chicago
International Art Exposition,
Navy Pier, Chicago, Illinois
"Visiting Artists," Lakeside
Studios, Lakeside, Michigan
"Visiting Artists," West Gallery,
Claremont Graduate School,
Claremont
"New Ways of Seeing," Marilyn
Pink Gallery, Los Angeles
"Art In The Halls, Part II," City
Hall, City of West Hollywood

1986

"Raku: Fifteen Southern Califor-
nia Ceramists," Peppers Gallery,
University of Redlands,
Redlands, California
"Showcase 86," California State
Polytechnic University, Pomona,
California
"Flower Show," Theater Gallery,
Design Center of Los Angeles
ARRTS Auction to benefit
Central American Refugee Cen-
ter, Oranges/Sardines Gallery,
Los Angeles

1985

"Anne Scott Plummer and Mar-
garet Allen: Recent Sculpture,"
Antelope Valley College Gallery,
Lancaster, California
"3 Ceramists," Theater Gallery,
Design Center of Los Angeles
"Love and Lace," Los Angeles
Contemporary Exhibitions
(LACE), Los Angeles
"Art Faculty Exhibition," Brand
Art Library, Glendale, California

1984

"Art in Clay: 1950s to 1980s in
Southern California," Barnsdall
Municipal Art Gallery,
Los Angeles

"9th International Biennale of
Ceramic Art in Vallauris," Hotel
de Ville, Vallauris, France
"Scripps Clay Connection, 40th
Scripps Ceramic Annual," Lang
Art Gallery, Scripps College,
Claremont
"Earth and Fire, Selections from
the Marer Collection," Mont-
gomery Art Gallery, Pomona
College, Claremont
"Cotton Exchange Show," Los
Angeles Contemporary Exhibi-
tions, Los Angeles
"30th Annual Juried Exhibition,"
San Diego Art Institute, San
Diego, California
"Ink and Clay," California State
Polytechnic University, Pomona
"Functional Ceramics,"
Functional Art, Beverly Hills,
California
"Robin," sculptural installation
for percussive performance,
Olio's, Los Angeles

1983

"Imaginative Sculpture," Gallery
at the Plaza, Security Pacific
National Bank, Los Angeles
"The Figurative Vessel," Garth
Clark Gallery, Los Angeles
"Westwood Clay National,"
Downey Museum of Art,
Downey
"Extensions," San Diego State
University Gallery, San Di[ego]
"Contemporary Trends,"
Antelope Valley College,
Lancaster
"Marer Collection Catal[og]
Benefit," Lang Art Galle[ry]
Scripps College, Claremo[nt]
"Silver Jubilee," Downey
Museum of Art, Downe[y]
"Alumni Exhibition and
Auction," Chrysalis Galle[ry]
Claremont

Collections

Dee Roy and Mary M. Jones
Collection, California State
Polytechnic University, Pomona,
California

Downey Art Museum, Downey,
California

Fred and Mary Marer
Collection, Galleries of the
Claremont Colleges,
Claremont, California

John Michael Kohler Arts Center,
Sheboygan, Wisconsin

Kohler Company, Kohler,
Wisconsin

Sun Valley Center of Arts and
Humanities, Sun Valley, Idaho

Vallauris International Museum
of Ceramics, Vallauris, France

Mr. and Mrs. Michael Cincola

Robert Corning

Stephane Janssen

David Koslow

Patti Pinaire

Matilda Rummage

Mr. and Mrs. Stephen Shirley

Sylvester Stallone